Teacher Quality

The Hoover Institution gratefully acknowledges the following individuals and foundations for their significant support of the

Initiative
on
American Public Education

KORET FOUNDATION
TAD AND DIANNE TAUBE
LYNDE AND HARRY BRADLEY FOUNDATION
BOYD AND JILL SMITH
JACK AND MARY LOIS WHEATLEY
FRANKLIN AND CATHERINE JOHNSON
JERRY AND PATTI HUME
DORIS AND DONALD FISHER
BERNARD LEE SCHWARTZ FOUNDATION

*The Hoover Institution
gratefully acknowledges generous support from*

KORET FOUNDATION

in the publication of this volume.

Teacher Quality

EDITED BY
Lance T. Izumi and Williamson M. Evers

HOOVER INSTITUTION PRESS
STANFORD UNIVERSITY
STANFORD, CALIFORNIA

PACIFIC RESEARCH INSTITUTE
SAN FRANCISCO, CALIFORNIA

The Pacific Research Institute for Public Policy (PRI), founded in
1979, promotes the cornerstones of a civil society—individual free-
dom and personal responsibility. PRI believes these principles are
best achieved through a free-market economy, limited government,
and private initiative. The Institute publishes original research in
four key areas—education, health and welfare, technology, and the
environment—and conducts strategic outreach to lawmakers, media,
business leaders, and mainstream audiences nationwide. Through
these comprehensive efforts, PRI is a leading force in "putting ideas
into action."

www.pacificresearch.org

Hoover Institution Press Publication No. 505

First printing 2002
07 06 05 04 03 02   9 8 7 6 5 4 3 2 1

Manufactured in the United States of America

The paper used in this publication meets the minimum requirements of
the American National Standard for Information Sciences—
Permanence of Paper for Printed Library Materials, ANSI Z39.48–1984.

Library of Congress Cataloging-in-Publication Data

Teacher quality / edited by Lance T. Izumi and Williamson M. Evers.
    p. cm.
  Includes bibliographical references and index.
    ISBN 0-8179-2932-0 (pbk.)
    1. Teachers—Training of—United States—Congresses. 2. Educational
accountability—United States—Congresses. I. Izumi, Lance T., 1958– II. Evers,
Williamson M., 1948– III. Hoover Institution on War, Revolution and Peace.

LB1715 .T426 2002
379.1'58'0973—dc21

                                                    2002068699

Contents

Foreword
John Raisian and Sally C. Pipes / *vii*

Preface: What Works in Teaching
William J. Bennett / *ix*

Introduction
Lance T. Izumi and Williamson M. Evers / *xiii*

Teacher Quality
Eric A. Hanushek / 1

Teacher Quality and Equity in Educational Opportunity:
Findings and Policy Implications
June C. Rivers and William L. Sanders / 13

Teacher Quality Accountability Systems:
The View from Pennsylvania
Eugene W. Hickok / 25

Teacher Training and Pedagogical Methods
J. E. Stone / 33

Teaching Methods
Herbert J. Walberg / 55

APPENDIX: CONFERENCE AGENDA / 73

EDITORS AND CONTRIBUTORS / 75

INDEX / 79

Foreword

Although education reform remains one of the top issues of our day, it is, in many ways, still one of the least understood. Too often, education discussions fail to address the tough problems that affect student performance, centering instead on tangential issues. For example, it is much easier for legislators to increase education spending on an array of programs—many of which have no empirical correlation to student achievement—than on reforming university schools of education, revamping teacher training, and improving teacher quality. Yet it is the latter that research shows will have the greatest impact on improving the performance of our students.

For this reason, the Hoover Institution and the Pacific Research Institute for Public Policy (PRI) convened a conference on teacher quality that addressed the critical issues of the effect of poorly prepared teachers on their students, the reform of the teacher education system, and the formulation of methods for making teachers accountable for their performance. The nation's leading experts gathered at the conference to present formal papers on various aspects of teacher quality. Education policy makers, legislative staff members, heads of education and philanthropic foundations, business leaders, academics and researchers, education media, and grassroots education activists attended. The conference was held at the Hoover Institution in May 2000.

The papers presented at the conference, which are contained in this publication, were catalysts for discussion and debate among conference participants. We believe that readers of these papers will react in similar fashion, and we hope that they will be spurred not only to think about these issues in new ways but also to then take steps to influence policy makers so that true reforms can be enacted.

Both the Hoover Institution and the PRI are greatly indebted to the Koret Foundation for its generous support of the project. Indeed, it was Koret's Tad Taube who first urged Hoover and the PRI to jointly put on the conference. That the conference turned out to be such a success and will have lasting impact on education policy is due in significant part to Mr. Taube and Koret's foresight and commitment.

The conference and this publication are among the many examples of cooperation between the Hoover Institution and the PRI. Hoover and the PRI are near each other geographically in Northern California, and together the two public policy research organizations can field an unmatched array of experts on a wide range of issues and subjects. Current joint projects include production of a coedited primer on K–12 education reform and collaboration between Hoover and PRI researchers on an analysis of state education-accountability systems. We believe that these and other joint projects will result in both organizations' increasing their ability to shape the public policy debate and to influence decisions and outcomes.

SALLY C. PIPES
President
Pacific Research Institute

JOHN RAISIAN
Director
Hoover Institution

Preface:
What Works in Teaching

William J. Bennett

The essential question of education policy is neither complex nor vague. In fact, it is quite simple: What works? This collection of research brought to you by the Pacific Research Institute and the Hoover Institution will do much to help schools—and parents—answer this question. The authors in this volume, some of the brightest minds in education research, have studied the most pressing questions about teacher quality and practices. They have reviewed thousands of education studies, closely examined state test scores, and explored education theories of the past thirty years in order to assess where we are—and where we ought to be.

In many cases, the authors' findings confirm common sense. William Sanders and June Rivers, for instance, demonstrate that nothing is as important to learning as the quality of a student's teacher. The difference between a good teacher and a bad teacher is so great that fifth-grade students who have poor teachers in grades three through five score roughly *50 percentile points* below similar groups of students who are fortunate enough to have effective teachers.

Oftentimes, however, the authors find conventional wisdom to be dead wrong. Eric Hanushek concludes that many of the things we normally believe produce good teachers—teacher training, a qualified academic background, stricter certification standards, and teacher testing—do not improve student test scores to any significant degree. It is for this reason that Hanushek encourages us to worry less about *what* makes a teacher successful and actually *do* more to *encourage* them to be successful. How? Develop a system that will reward and honor good teachers. Given the job they do, these teachers deserve as much praise, thanks, and honor as any American citizen.

Overall, the papers provide the reader with a portrait of a good teacher and good teaching methods. As Herb Walberg properly concludes in his paper, "Effective teaching methods hardly seem a mystery. . . . The mystery seems to be why such principles are not already in place." Our task thus becomes putting such principles in place—to set high standards for teachers, to develop strong accountability systems for measuring performance, and to reward those who perform and frown upon those who do not.

We know what works. And we must now turn our attention to forming policies that reflect what we know. There are many people dedicated to protecting the status quo, including some people who would seem to be natural allies of improving schools. The heads of both major teachers' unions recently rejected the idea of merit pay for teachers. They continue to oppose the movement for standards and accountability. We should remember, however, that teachers exist for the sake of the students and that good teachers have nothing to fear from thoughtful education reform.

To paraphrase Oliver Wendell Holmes, the teacher who is great is the teacher who makes others believe in greatness. Teaching is more than "facilitating the acquisition of skills." It is offering an invitation and encouragement to life, to a fulfilled life.

As we move forward, we must be determined and vigilant. The American people have invested enormous amounts of money in the education system—and have entrusted it with their children. With this in mind, we must ensure that the system provides the best possible education for kids. This report from the Pacific Research Institute and the Hoover Institution will help support that critical process.

Introduction

Lance T. Izumi and Williamson M. Evers

In May 2000, the Pacific Research Institute for Public Policy (PRI) and the Hoover Institution cosponsored a conference at Stanford on teacher quality that brought together some of the nation's top experts on the subject. Why teacher quality? With education reform at the forefront of recent political debate, a wide array of programs aimed at increasing student performance have been proposed and adopted. From reducing class size to changing curricula to increasing funding, lawmakers and education officials have been trying to find, often in vain, the silver bullet that will raise test scores and student learning. These quick-fix solutions, however, not only fail to address the public education system's core problems but also usually have little or no basis in empirical research. For example, evidence shows little improvement in student performance as a result of states' spending billions of dollars on class-size reduction. What the research does show is that the quality of classroom teachers has the greatest impact on the performance levels of students. High-quality teachers using proven teaching methodologies produce high-achieving students.

Despite this well-documented fact, the subject of improving teacher quality is often, and sadly, absent from education policy discussions. Where teacher improvement programs have been implemented, they are often little more than watered-down public-relations schemes aimed at assuring the public that something is being done. In reality, largely, the status quo is being maintained. For instance, teacher peer-review programs, although popular with politicians and teacher unions, have proven ineffective in improving teacher quality and weeding out poor-performing teachers. In contrast, a true teacher improvement program would focus on key indicators, including teacher assessment, effective teaching methodologies, and performance incentive systems.

The PRI-Hoover conference sought to define and outline these factors. Each of the presenters used his or her special expertise to identify the various problems in the area of teacher quality and what must be done in order to craft a comprehensive teacher-improvement strategy and agenda.

Professor Herb Walberg, one of the nation's leading authorities on international education data, provides a fleshed-out context for the discussion of teacher quality by using a variety of indicators to compare American public education with its counterparts in the industrialized world. He finds that, among other things, American students spend less time studying, work less at home on schoolwork, and spend less time reading. Such factors correlate directly with the level of student performance. Walberg recommends tough academic content standards and a change in teaching practices to adopt proven methodologies, such as direct instruction.

Hoover Institution fellow Dr. Eric Hanushek, perhaps the country's top education economist, discusses what does and does not affect student performance. For example, he finds that more education spending does not correlate with increased student achievement. How money is spent, rather than how much is spent, is more important. And what most affects student performance is the quality of the teacher in the classroom.

Dr. June Rivers and Dr. William L. Sanders, formerly of the University of Tennessee, reveal just how much student performance is affected by teacher quality. Employing an innovative value-added methodology, Rivers and Sanders use student assessment devices to determine the quality of teachers. Controlling for a range of factors, Rivers and Sanders find that the quality of teachers is highly variable and that having consecutive years of good or bad teachers can have a dramatic effect, positive or negative, on student achievement.

Dr. Eugene Hickok, former Pennsylvania Secretary of Education, now U.S. Undersecretary of Education, describes what a model teacher-quality program should look like. Along with his boss in Pennsylvania, Governor Tom Ridge, Hickok designed a program that emphasizes holding schools of education accountable, requiring preassessment and postassessment of teachers who take professional development courses, and focusing on the real knowledge and quality of teacher applicants as opposed to paper credentials. Recently passed by the Pennsylvania legislature, the Ridge-Hickok program offers a roadmap for other states seeking to improve teacher quality.

Dr. J. E. Stone, a leading critic of current teacher education programs, focuses on the disconnect between the demands of education consumers (parents and taxpayers) for increased student achievement and the downplaying of such achievement by education providers, such as schools of education and teachers. He recommends a wholesale revamping of teacher education that stresses basic academics, teacher assessments, and teaching methodologies based on empirical research rather than voguish psychology or pedagogy.

Although teacher quality is the most important factor in improving student performance, it is also the most difficult to affect. Schools of education, teacher unions, the existing teacher workforce, state governments, and local school boards are just some of the players who have an impact on teacher quality. Changing teacher preparation, teaching methodologies, teacher incentives, and other key teacher quality factors is a monumental undertaking. However, if policy makers are truly serious about improving the achievement and learning of students, then this is a challenge they must confront head on. The papers presented here should give policy makers clear guidance for meeting this challenge.

The editors are indebted to this book's authors for writing their chapters and participating in the conference on teacher quality. We are also indebted to the directors of the Pacific Research Institute and the Hoover Institution—Sally Pipes and John Raisian, respectively—for bringing us together in this joint endeavor. The book and conference owe their existence to the generous support of the Koret Foundation and the interest of its president, Tad Taube. Thomas Dawson III, then of the Pacific Research Institute, now at the U.S. Department of Education, helped keep track of the manuscripts during the editing process. We are also indebted to the editorial staff of the Hoover Institution Press, in particular, Pat Baker, Ann Wood, and Joan D. Saunders, for their efforts in putting the book in final form.

Teacher Quality

Eric A. Hanushek

Dr. Eric Hanushek, the nation's foremost education economist, addresses one of the most important questions in education policy—by what means can government improve the quality of the nation's teacher force, and how can it accomplish that goal without making the current problems worse? Hanushek's basic answer is that government should not prescribe solutions for local schools, but focus instead on providing incentives. According to Hanushek, "If the objective is to improve student performance, student performance should be the focal point of policy."

In the past, government has relied on regulations that determine education inputs, for example, class size and credentials. Rather than boosting student performance, these mandates have often had perverse effects. Shrinking class size increases the demand for teachers, while credentialing requirements, which do not ensure quality, limit the supply of candidates. The combined effect is that the teachers the school districts end up hiring are often low-performing.

Other variables, like differences in teacher ability, have far greater impact on student performance yet have largely been ignored by government. For example, teachers who elicit academic gains from their students are not rewarded for their achievements. Most teachers are hard-working and doing the best they can, but in the absence of incentives to improve, additional resources are not directed to maximizing student output. Hanushek argues that the adoption of performance incentives, while also holding schools and teachers accountable for the choices they make, is crucial if student achievement is to improve.

School reform is a topic on many people's minds today, and the air is full of advice and recommendations. Unlike many policy areas, the vast majority of people have strongly held opinions, mostly arising from their own personal experiences in school. As a result, much of policy making involves walking a line between research findings and popular views. Unfortunately, these popular views frequently are not the best guide for decision making.

This discussion begins with some evidence about the importance of teacher quality and moves to ideas about how the quality of teachers can be improved. Central to all of the discussion is the relationship between incentives and accountability. In simplest terms, if the objective is to improve student performance, student performance should be the focal point of policy.

From a policy perspective, although the proper role for different levels of government has been controversial, I believe that there are important things to be done by the federal government. These things are, nonetheless, quite different from both the current activities and many of the things that are being discussed.

THE IMPORTANCE OF TEACHER QUALITY

Starting with the Coleman Report, the monumental investigation in 1966 by the Office of Education, many have argued that schools do not matter and that only families and peers affect performance. Part of this view is true, and part is quite wrong. This report was the most extensive investigation of schools *ever* undertaken. Unfortunately, that report and subsequent interpretations of it have generally confused "measurability" with true effects. Specifically, characteristics of schools and classrooms, like the teacher having a master's degree or the class size being small, did not show any effect on student performance—leading to the conclusion that schools do not matter. This conclusion, probably more than anything else, led to a prevailing view that differences among schools are not very important.

The extensive research over the past 35 years has led to two clear conclusions. First, there are very important differences among teachers. This finding, of course, does not surprise many parents, who are well aware of quality differences of teachers. Second, these differences are not captured by common measures of teachers (qualifications, experience, and the like). This latter finding has important implications that I sketch below.

The magnitude of differences in teachers is impressive. Let me provide two different indications of teacher quality. For these measures I use a simple definition of teacher quality: good teachers are ones who get large gains in student achievement for their classes; bad teachers are just the opposite. Looking at the range of quality for teachers within a single large urban district, teachers near the top of the quality distribution can get an entire year's worth of additional learning out of their students compared to those near the bottom. That is, a good teacher will get a gain of one and a half grade-level equivalents, whereas a bad teacher will get a gain of only half a year for a single academic year. Alternatively, if we look at just the variations in performance resulting from differences in teacher quality within a typical school, then moving from an average teacher to one at the 85th percentile of teacher quality would imply that the better teacher's students would move up more than 7 percentile rankings in the year.

We can also return to the popular argument that family background is overwhelmingly important and that schools cannot be expected to make up for bad preparation from home. The latter estimates of teacher performance suggest that having three years of good teachers (85th percentile) in a row would overcome the average achievement deficit between low-income kids (those on free or reduced-price lunch) and others. In other words, high-quality teachers can make up for the typical deficits that we see in the preparation of kids from disadvantaged backgrounds.

Unfortunately, the current school system does not ensure any streaks of such high-quality teachers. In fact, it is currently as likely that the typical student gets a run of bad teachers—with the symmetric achievement losses—as a run of good teachers. Altering this situation is the school policy issue, in my mind.

CERTIFICATION AND OTHER CENTRAL APPROACHES TO QUALITY

In recognition of the importance of quality teachers, a variety of recommendations and policy initiatives have been introduced. Unfortunately, the currently most popular ones are likely to lower teacher quality rather than improve it.

The idea that has been picked up by policy makers at all levels is to increase the requirements to become a teacher. The idea is simple: if we can insist on better prepared and more able teachers, teacher quality will necessarily rise and student performance will respond. This argument—at least as implemented—proves as incorrect as it is simple.

The range of options being pushed forward include raising the course work requirement for teacher certification, testing teachers on either general or specific knowledge, requiring specific kinds of undergraduate degrees, and requiring master's degrees. Each of these has surface plausibility, but little evidence exists to suggest that these are strongly related to teacher quality and to student achievement.

More pernicious, these requirements almost certainly act to reduce the supply of teachers. In other words, the proposed requirements do little or nothing to ensure high-quality teachers, and at the same time, they cut down on the number of people who might enter teaching. Teacher certification requirements are generally promoted as ensuring that there is a floor on quality, but if they end up keeping out high-quality teachers who do not want to take the specific required courses, such requirements act more like a ceiling on quality.

The story on teacher certification initiatives is actually just a special case of a larger set of misguided policies that go under the name "input policies." These are attempts to specify pieces of the educational process. The recent craze for lowering class size—two years in a row the federal budget was held up until agreement could be reached on federal funding for hiring new teachers so that class sizes could be reduced—is the clearest example of an input policy: a variety of motivations have pushed this policy, which has little chance of success in terms of student achievement. This actually typifies the most common kinds of policies that we have been undertaking for the last three decades at least.

The Evidence on Inputs

The evidence on each of the input policy issues comes from a variety of sources but is very consistent. The simplest version is that we have been pursuing these policies for decades, and they have not worked. Table 1 shows the pattern of resources devoted to U.S. education since 1960. There have been dramatic increases in just the resources that people today advocate supplying. If we concentrate on the period of 1970 through 1995 (because we have student performance measures for a comparable period), we see that pupil-teacher ratios have fallen by

TABLE 1   Public School Resources in the United States, 1960–1995

Resource	Pupil-teacher ratio	Percentage of teachers with master's or other higher degree	Median years of teacher experience	Current expenditure/ADA (1996–1997 dollars)
1960	25.8	23.5	11	$2,122
1970	22.3	27.5	8	$3,645
1980	18.7	49.6	12	$4,589
1990	17.2	53.1	15	$6,239
1995	17.3	56.2	15	$6,434

close to a quarter, the number of teachers master's degrees has more than doubled, and median teacher experience has almost doubled. Because each of these inputs costs more, average real spending per pupil has increased by more than 75 percent, that is, by three-quarters after allowing for inflation. But if we look at student performance on the National Assessment of Educational Progress, we see that performance is virtually unchanged in math and reading and has fallen in science. This is hardly what the proponents of increased resources suggest should have happened.

This evidence on resources and performance is supported by detailed econometric studies. These statistical analyses of what goes on in the classroom provide little reason to believe that input policies will systematically improve student outcomes. While some studies suggest positive relationships with added resources, they are balanced by studies that actually show negative relationships. The existence of some positive findings allows advocates of specific policies to point to highly selective evidence supporting their cause, but it does not make for a different reality.

Similarly, with the recent push for class-size reduction, considerable attention has been focused on the Tennessee experiment of the 1980s, Project STAR. A much larger amount of uncertainty surrounds the evidence from this than most advocates want to acknowledge. Without going too far afield here, suffice it to say that Project STAR has been hugely overinterpreted. The clearest indication from this experiment is that very large reductions in class size (from 23 to 15) lead to small effects on student performance in kindergarten—hardly the evidence needed to support small reductions in class size at all grade levels.

The Policy Implications

It is important to understand how pursuing the conventional input policies could actually hurt the situation. As pointed out, increasing the requirements for teacher certification could limit the supply of potential teachers and could thereby actually lower the quality of the typical teacher who ends up in the classroom. Similarly, lowering class size could hurt in two ways. First, it is very expensive, so it absorbs funds that could be applied to productive policies. Second, it expands the demand for teachers and can lower student achievement if the quality of new teachers ends up lower. Note, however, that we do not know much about the overall effects. The California class-size-reduction policy of 1997 indeed drew in more teachers who were not fully certified, but whether they were lower quality is unclear because certification is not closely related to effective performance in the classroom.

The generic issue is whether or not higher levels of government can effectively improve schools through uniform funding or with rules for how education is to be conducted in local schools. Here the evidence is quite clear. We do not know how to identify a well-defined set of inputs that is either necessary or sufficient for ensuring high-quality schooling. Finding such a set has been the Holy Grail of education research, and the search has been quite unsuccessful. Indeed, I do not believe that it is an issue of just needing more or better research. I simply do not think that we will identify (at least within our lifetimes) such a set with any clarity. I believe that the educational process is much too complicated for us to uncover a small set of criteria that are amenable to central legislation and control.

The evidence also underscores an aspect of the policy-making problem. Class-size reductions have been politically very popular. The federal government was merely mimicking the popular 1997 actions of the state of California. A large part of the political sentiment emanates from the commonsense arguments that persuade the general public that these are sensible policies. They just conflict with the evidence. And they imply that the policy maker must deal with political problems as well as policy problems.

PERFORMANCE INCENTIVES—
AN ATTRACTIVE ALTERNATIVE

The simple position taken here is: *if one is concerned about student performance, one should gear policy to student performance.* Perhaps the largest problem with the current organization of schools is that nobody's job or career is closely related to student performance. Relatedly, popular input policies do nothing to change the structure of incentives. The key to effective policy is turning to performance incentives for teachers and other school personnel.

This is not to say that teachers or other school personnel are currently misbehaving. I personally think that most teachers are very hard working and that the vast majority are trying to do the best they can in the classroom. It is simply a statement that they are responding to the incentives that are placed in front of them (just as we all do). So when various decisions are being made, such as how to deal with added resources, the decisions may or may not be directed at the use that would maximize student learning. Instead, they might be directed at things that are publicly popular or things that make the decision makers' job easier or more pleasant.

The problem that goes along with this position statement is that we do not know the best way to structure incentives. We have not tried many performance incentive systems, so we have very little experience with or evidence from them.

A variety of approaches have been suggested and have conceptual appeal: merit pay for teachers, rewards to high-performing schools, and various forms of choice, including charter schools, tax rebates, and vouchers. Although evidence is slowly accumulating, the range of experiences is very limited.

There are nonetheless some things that we are quite certain about in the design of incentive structures.

Accountability and Value Added

One reason for general teacher resistance to incentive systems like merit pay is concern about what is being rewarded.

We know that families make a huge difference in the education of students. An implication of this is that we should not reward or punish teachers for the education they are not responsible for. If some students come to school better prepared than others, their teachers should not receive extra rewards. Similarly, if students come from disadvantaged backgrounds that leave them less well-prepared for school, we should not punish their teachers.

We want to reward teachers for what they add to a student's learning, that is, for their value added to the education of the child. Rewards should be geared to what teachers control, not to the specific group of students that they are given.

Pursuing this approach requires an aggressive system of performance measurement. We have to be able to track the progress of individual students, and we have to be able to relate this progress to the teachers who are responsible for it. This does not necessarily mean that we want a system of individual rewards as opposed to group rewards for teachers in a school, but it does mean that we have to accurately measure the performance of schools. This area—designing accountability systems—is an obvious area for federal leadership (although not necessarily for federal control).

Local Decision Making

It is also almost inconceivable that we could run a good performance incentive system from the national capital or even a state capital. If we try to devise the one best system and force it on local districts and schools, we will almost certainly fail. This statement really bites strongest when thinking about the limits of the federal government. Whereas the federal government can help provide funding for and guidance on the use of performance incentives, it is not in a good position to determine the "how" of the performance incentives.

At the same time, we should not simply assume that local districts and schools are currently able to make good decisions. Personnel have not now been chosen for their ability to operate and manage different incentive systems. And, as mentioned, we do not have sufficient experience to provide any detailed guidance. Nonetheless, preparing local officials for performing these tasks is where we should be headed.

Neither should we assume that all policies that emphasize student outcomes and that provide performance incentives are altogether good. The design of incentives is complicated because many incentive structures lead to unintended and undesirable consequences. For example, if a move to broaden school choice led to complete racial or economic segregation in the schools, we would not think that it was a desirable policy. Therefore, we need to develop more experience with incentives and to evaluate these experiences. With incentive systems, the details generally prove to be critical.

LEARNING ABOUT INCENTIVES

In my opinion, one of the largest problems with education policy is that we never learn much from the policies we put into place. In fact, we frequently make policy decisions in ways that defy *ever* learning about their effects. The California class size initiative is a good example. All districts in the same state were simultaneously given financial incentives to reduce class size. Thus, even if one looks at student performance around the state, it is not possible to see what would happen in the absence of these incentives. Similarly, England recently introduced a broad policy of merit pay for teachers, but they did it everywhere at once. If student performance changes, is it because of the new incentives or because of other factors?

I realize that it is not the kind of policy that brings immediate political gratification, but I believe that nothing would have a more powerful influence on student performance ten years from now than a broad program of educational experimentation. The parallel with medicine is painfully obvious. In medicine, we are willing to admit that we do not know everything about different procedures or therapies, and we conduct random-assignment controlled experiments to identify the effectiveness of different approaches. The results of this on the overall health of our population are clear and obvious. We also have a long history of social experimentation in health, welfare, and housing. We have learned an enormous amount over time that has helped to improve public policies. Nothing similar has occurred in education.

Experimentation and evaluation are legitimate federal roles. All states learn from these efforts, and no state takes into account the fact that evaluation results are useful to others. Without federal involvement there is likely to be too little investment in evaluation and knowledge production. Let me emphasize, however, that federal information collection is not the same as federal control of the schools, and there is no reason to expect that more centralized decision making would result from the federal government taking on a leadership role.

The problem, of course, is that experimentation and educational evaluation are not policies with mass appeal. Nonetheless, if we are to weed out bad policies and replace them with good policies, we need to accumulate evidence about performance.

CONCLUSIONS

Let me summarize.

1. Teacher quality is the key to improved schools.
2. Teacher quality cannot be readily linked to teacher characteristics; therefore, new and more extensive certification and training standards are unlikely to be effective.
3. Policies aimed at student performance instead of inputs offer the only real hope for improvement. Input policies, even though frequently popular, need to be resisted. At the same time, developing good accountability

systems is central, and the federal government can provide leadership (without nationalizing the process).

4. The federal government should limit its role to concerns of equity and of knowledge and should not attempt to act like a local school board. At the same time, the federal government should require performance for funds it disperses, such as the Title 1 funds that aid the education of disadvantaged students.

5. Developing improved policy requires better information about what works, and the most effective way of accumulating this evidence is the design of systematic experiments and evaluation.

Teacher Quality and Equity in Educational Opportunity: Findings and Policy Implications

June C. Rivers and William L. Sanders

In the following piece, Dr. June C. Rivers and her husband, Dr. William L. Sanders, both formerly of the University of Tennessee, describe how teachers can be evaluated based on the academic gains students make in their classrooms. Since 1992, these two statistical pioneers have annually compiled standardized test scores for approximately six million Tennessee children in a variety of academic fields. Along with test score information, data are collected on a wide range of student variables, including ethnicity.

This innovative approach allows student progress to be assessed from year to year, without controlling for external influences like poverty and family conditions. The longitudinal approach allows each student to serve as his or her own control, and empirical studies of the early results showed these analyses to be virtually unbiased by these external influences. Testing is sustained and consistent, which allows them to track what academic gains individual students make from one year to the next, regardless of the background of the children. Thus, teachers are considered as effective if they elicit appropriate gains for their students.

The findings have been provocative. Differences in teacher ability are substantial, and if students are assigned to consecutive ineffective teachers, the impact on student achievement in the short and long terms can be devastating. Most important, successful teachers can elicit significant gains from students of all ethnicities and income levels. This value-added model has potential to revolutionize how teacher quality is assessed, using objective measures to evaluate teachers.

INTRODUCTION

"Equity in education" is not a new phrase but one that has a diversity of meanings in educational policy circles. The different meanings of equity are accompanied by disagreements as to both the definition and the measurement of it. To some, equity in educational delivery will be achieved only when simple group averages across various demographic subgroups are equal. This simplistic definition of equity has resulted in huge debates and disagreements, ranging from accusations of ethnic biases in the measurement process (or instruments) to the argument that having all students at the same academic attainment level at the same time is an unrealistic expectation for educators. However, one definition of equity avoids much of this debate and allows for a more realistic measurement process to be put in place.

If true equity is defined as each student making appropriate academic growth each year, then expectations for *educators and students* can be set in terms of academic growth rates. The results of newer research indicate that the academic growth rate of student populations is primarily a function of the effectiveness of school districts, schools, and, most important, teachers. If appropriate rates of academic growth are sustained across grades, then *all* students' academic attainment will be ratcheted to higher levels. The achievement levels of second- and third-graders are not nearly as important as their attainment levels when they are eleventh- and twelfth-graders. Measurement methodology that separates educational influences from a multitude of possible confounding biases provides realistic diagnostic feedback for educators. Practice informed by appropriate measurement ensures that all students have opportunities to reach their full potential.

Tennessee Value-Added Assessment System

The Tennessee Value-Added Assessment System (TVAAS) is one statewide system that measures the impact that districts, schools, and teachers have on academic growth rates of student populations. The TVAAS database contains approximately six million student achievement test records from 1991 to the present. The individual student information was linked to specific teachers in 1994, allowing estimation of teacher effectiveness.[1]

The TVAAS accommodates learning indicators from a variety of tests, both multiple-choice and those requiring open-ended responses. To be included, tests must have high repeatability and strong correlation with curricular objectives, and they must also allow for sufficient discrimination at the extremes of the achievement spectrum.[2]

The TVAAS applies statistical mixed model methodology to a longitudinal database that has been created from Tennessee's testing regime, which measures each student each year in five subjects. The educational influences on academic gain are estimated from a multivariate longitudinal model that uses all information for each student, no matter how sparse or complete. With this methodology, the TVAAS avoids many of the problems that have traditionally barred the use of achievement data in assessing effectiveness of schools and teachers; with the TVAAS, (1) exogenous influences are separated from test performance because students are allowed to serve as their own controls; (2) longitudinal analysis across years with repeated measures across subjects improves the efficiency of the estimates of the model parameters; (3) all available data are used and no imputation techniques are required; (4) at the teacher level, estimation of shrinkage protects against fortuitous misclassification. The TVAAS database allows exploration of the effect of the teacher's impact on student achievement.[3]

---

[1]William L. Sanders, A. M. Saxton, and S. P. Horn, "The Tennessee Value-Added Assessment System: A Quantitative, Outcomes-Based Approach to Educational Assessment" in *Grading Teachers, Grading Schools*, edited by J. Millman, Thousand Oaks, Calif.: Corwin Press, Inc., 1997.

[2]Ibid.

[3]Ibid.

Pertinent Findings from the University of Tennessee Value-Added Research and Assessment Center

Many research findings from the TVAAS, replicated by other researchers, are pertinent to the issue of teacher quality. The major findings summarized here may be useful for policy makers as they attempt to provide equitable opportunities for all students.

- The effect of teachers can be separated from ethnic, socioeconomic, and parental influences.[4]
- The variability of teacher effectiveness increases across grades and is most pronounced in mathematics.[5]
- In the extreme, fifth-grade students experiencing highly ineffective teachers in grades three through five scored about 50 percentile points below their peers of comparable previous achievement who were fortunate enough to experience highly effective teachers for those same grades.[6]
- A teacher's effect on student achievement is measurable at least four years after students have left the tutelage of that teacher.[7]

---

[4]D. A. Harville, "A Review of the Tennessee Value-Added Assessment System (TVAAS)" (manuscript, Iowa State University, 1995); H. R. Jordan, R. L. Mendro, and D. Weerasinghe, "Teacher Effects on Longitudinal Student Achievement" (paper presented at the National Evaluation Institute, Indianapolis, Ind., 1997); William L. Sanders and S. Horn, "Educational Assessment Reassessed: The Usefulness of Standardized and Alternative Measures of Student Achievement as Indicators for the Assessment of Educational Outcomes" in *Educational Policy Analysis Archives* 3, no. 6; Sanders, Saxton, and Horn, "Tennessee Value-Added Assessment System."

[5]University of Tennessee Value-Added Research and Assessment Center, *Graphical Summary of Educational Findings from the Tennessee Value-Added Assessment System (TVAAS) 1995* (Knoxville: University of Tennessee Value-Added Research and Assessment Center, 1995).

[6]Jordan, Mendro, and Weerasinghe, "Teacher Effects"; William L. Sanders and June C. Rivers, "Cumulative and Residual Effects of Teachers on Future Student Academic Achievement: Research Progress Report" (Knoxville: University of Tennessee Value-Added Research and Assessment Center, 1996).

[7]June C. Rivers-Sanders, "The Impact of Teacher Effect on Student Math Competency Achievement" (Ed.D. diss., University of Tennessee, 1999); Sanders and Rivers, *Cumulative and Residual Effects of Teachers.*

- When a student has experienced an ineffective teacher or a series of ineffective teachers, there is little evidence of a compensatory effect provided by experiencing more effective ones in later years.[8]
- Regardless of ethnicity, children of similar previous achievement levels tend to respond similarly to an individual teacher.[9]
- Within two Tennessee metropolitan districts, children of color were overrepresented in less effective teachers' classrooms by about 10 percent and underrepresented in highly effective teachers' classrooms by about 10 percent.[10]
- Teachers who are relatively ineffective tend to be ineffective with all student subgroups across the prior achievement spectrum, whereas teachers who are highly effective tend to be very effective with all student subgroups across the same spectrum.[11]
- The effect of the teacher far overshadows classroom variables, such as previous achievement level of students, class size as it is currently operationalized, heterogeneity of students, and the ethnic and socioeconomic makeup of the classroom.[12]
- In the extreme, for students scoring in the lowest quartile in fourth-grade math, the probability of passing an eighth-grade-level test (required for high school graduation) ranged from 15 to 60 percent as a function of the sequence of teachers and how effective they were. Students in this achievement group experiencing four teachers of average effectiveness had a 38 percent probability for passing the test.[13]

---

[8]Sanders and Rivers, *Cumulative and Residual Effects of Teachers.*
[9]Ibid.
[10]Ibid.
[11]Ibid.
[12]S. P. Wright, S. P. Horn, and William L. Sanders, "Teachers and Classroom Context Effects on Student Achievement: Implications for Teacher Evaluation" in *Journal of Personnel Evaluation in Education* 11, no. 1, 57–67.
[13]June C. Rivers-Sanders, "Impact of Teacher Effect on Math Achievement."

- In the extreme, students testing between the 25th percentile and the 50th percentile in the fourth grade who also experienced a series of highly effective teachers in grades five through eight could be expected to pass the high-stakes test with a probability of about 80 percent; their peers of comparable previous achievement unfortunate enough to have experienced four very ineffective teachers in the same grades could be expected to pass the same test with a probability of about 40 percent. A sequence of four teachers of average effectiveness offered students within this prior achievement level a probability of passing of about 60 percent.[14]

DISCUSSION

The cumulative and residual effects of teachers on the academic progress of students are huge. Collectively, these research findings paint a vivid picture of the extreme variability of teachers' effectiveness and the dramatic effect this variability has on student progress. The starkness of this picture suggests three critical areas of policy implication if school districts are to provide *equity in education:*

1. School districts must have a measurement system that allows them to monitor the variability among schools and teachers and an adequate means of communicating the measurement.
2. School districts must shrink the variability in effectiveness among existing teachers.
3. When school districts assign students to teachers, districts must minimize possible teacher effectiveness inequities for students.

Measuring Schooling Effects

Within their budgetary constraints, policy makers must determine the most effective way to provide robust and unbi-

---

[14]Ibid.

ased measurement. Unless educators receive meaningful measurement, they will continue to disavow measures of effectiveness that focus only on such convoluted and biased measures of student attainment as ethnicity, socioeconomic status, and parental influences. In the absence of unbiased measures of student progress, the disgruntled voice of all teachers, inappropriately evaluated, will continue to protect those teachers who are truly ineffective, making it very difficult to assist the latter in improving their classroom practices.

Based on what has been learned about teacher effectiveness and teacher effectiveness sequences, measurement and related reporting should serve two purposes, each requiring varying degrees of conservatism—accountability and diagnosis. Sophisticated statistical and computing techniques allow an integrated delivery of the two from the same testing regime. Much debate focuses on the types of testing instruments to be deployed. However, it appears that having measures of student achievement annually is more crucial than using a particular type of instrument,[15] provided that the three previously mentioned conditions are met (strong repeatability, high correlation between the test and curricular objectives, and sufficient stretch for discriminating on both ends of the achievement spectrum). Local districts have a range of choices in obtaining the desired test data, but economic constraints may determine what is locally optimal. Consider, for instance, this scenario: testing occurs *only* in grades three and eight in mathematics; students at the eighth-grade level do not reach the attainment level mandated by the local board of education. It is highly improbable that schools and teachers would be able to accurately assess where between grades four and eight the incidence or incidences of inadequate progress occurred. This testing regime that includes only data from grades three and eight does not have the diagnostic sensitivity of an annual testing program.

Reporting by TVAAS is an example of integrated delivery of accountability and diagnostic information from the same testing regime. Tennessee began testing students in grades

---

[15]Sanders and Horn, "Educational Assessment Reassessed."

two through eight in math, reading, language arts, science, and social studies in 1991. Data from these administrations; writing assessment data for grades four, seven, and eleven; and high school end-of-course math tests are analyzed to produce district, school, and teacher reporting. Multiple indicators for each student increase the sensitivity provided from any one measurement.

The official TVAAS reporting for accountability purposes provides districts and schools with three years of estimates of means and gain for each subject and grade served by the district and school, and this reporting provides teachers with three years of estimated student gain for each of their subject-grade combinations. The three years of data are averaged to provide the progress indicator used for accountability. Additionally, the district and school reporting provides an estimate of the percentage of progress the average student would be expected to make across grades when compared to the average student from the national norming sample. This estimate of percent of cumulative norm gain is the progress indicator for determining the effectiveness or ineffectiveness of either a school or a district. The minimal expectation for districts and schools is that enrolled children make at least enough progress to maintain their position relevant to their peers of comparable prior achievement. A school with a 100 percent cumulative norm gain is meeting this minimal target. Students in a 120th percentile school are progressing at a rate that will put them at an attainment level one grade beyond that of their peers of comparable prior achievement, when the 120th percentage rate is maintained across grades three through eight.

Additionally, a less conservative reporting series for districts and schools provides simple paired mean gains for various prior achievement subgroups. For this report, students are placed in prior achievement groupings based on their standing within the district. A student's standing is determined by averaging the two most recent years of data for a particular subject. The mean gains for each subgroup are provided. This report is especially useful in monitoring the availability of equitable learning opportunities for students with various levels of prior achievement because the disaggregation by prior achievement allows the user to compare the subgroup mean gain to the target gain. Subgroup means below the target reflect less than adequate progress, whereas subgroup means at or above the target imply that students are progressing at more desirable rates.

Shrinking Teacher Variability

Another concern of policy makers is to determine what is needed in order to shrink the variability in teacher effectiveness. Decreasing the variability will help ensure that fewer children have an ineffective teacher. Ineffective teachers cause learning consequences for students that are compounded when the frequency of ineffective teaching increases. Although *most* students do not experience teacher quality sequences at either of the extremes, many children, unfortunately, lack the benefit of effective teaching at some point in their K–12 years. The effect is insidious, causing underachievement each year they encounter an ineffective teacher until the cumulative effect becomes extremely visible in later grades. For example, some students complete algebra in the eighth grade, whereas others of similar prior achievement levels in early grades struggle with anything beyond the most remedial mathematics at the conclusion of their elementary years.

Policies for decreasing the variability of teacher effectiveness must address two areas: (1) identification through measurement and (2) professional development. Many teachers do not recognize that they are ineffective until confronted with the objective evidence that their students are not making appropriate rates of gain. Once they recognize their students' lack of progress, many tend to self-correct their teaching practices. Those with pedagogical weaknesses and others may require assistance through strategically planned professional development in order to learn to teach more effectively.

Minimizing the Impact of Ineffective Teachers

The existing policies for placing students with teachers deserve serious study to ensure that various subpopulations of prior achievement are not being subjected to systematic inequity across grades because they are assigned systematically to less effective teachers. For example, where do beginning teachers typically get assigned within a district? In larger districts, beginning teachers generally begin their employment in inner-city schools and seek transfers in assignment when they gain experience. Current TVAAS research suggests that teachers' effectiveness increases dramatically each year during the first ten years of teaching. If beginning teachers are disproportionately assigned to a school within a district, the children who have these teachers quite possibly are not receiving an opportunity to get a good education. Without some measurement of teacher effectiveness, this situation may be difficult to address.

Even though schools may be assisting less effective teachers to become more effective, principals should make a conscientious effort to avoid assigning students to multiple ineffective teachers in succession. Students unfortunate enough to encounter two or more ineffective teachers in sequence show measurably retarded academic growth. The effects on students' attitudes from having several ineffective teachers in a row have not been quantified; we need more research in this area. All children deserve to have highly effective teachers every year, but until something can be done to shrink the variability, no child deserves to experience two very ineffective teachers in a row.

CONCLUSION

Improving teacher quality is the mutual responsibility of educators and policy makers. Sophisticated measurement of teacher effectiveness is critical to this process because it ensures that teachers are evaluated fairly and provides diagnostic information for improving teacher effectiveness. When teachers understand that they are evaluated on their ability to facilitate progress for their students, their perception of the fairness of this evaluation should increase the likelihood that they will explore and implement ways to improve their teaching practices. And the fairness issue aside, the sensitivity of more sophisticated measurement provides better diagnostic information on which to base programmatic decisions. It brings a focus to these efforts that less sensitive measures fail to provide. With this more finely tuned metric, teachers and administrators are in a better position to ensure that all students have appropriate learning opportunities. Improving teacher quality will help ensure that more students reach their potential because they benefited from effective teachers *every* year.

Teacher Quality Accountability Systems: The View from Pennsylvania

Eugene W. Hickok

Dr. Eugene W. Hickok is one of the nation's leading authorities on teacher-quality accountability systems. As Pennsylvania's Secretary of Education for six years in the administration of Governor Tom Ridge, he was responsible for implementing an ambitious agenda aimed at providing more choice and flexibility for children enrolled in failing school districts. He has also led the way in strengthening teacher preparation and professional development programs by emphasizing accountability and the impact on student performance. His speech focused on the lessons he has learned in Pennsylvania and how they are applicable elsewhere.

"How do we find good teachers?" is a broad question. Not only must we find good teachers, but we must also prepare them to be effective in the classroom. We must retain good teachers as well and ensure they perform at high levels, and when they do not, we must deal with incompetents.

Professor Eric Hanushek has done extensive research on that silver bullet of all education reforms, smaller class sizes. And what have we found? Well, as he noted, class-size reduction is not all it's cracked up to be. Indeed, the quality of the teaching a child receives is a far greater determinant of student performance, whereas class size may or may not be a factor. Indeed, the experience with class size suggests a fundamental

---

This chapter presents edited excerpts from his conference speech.

problem we encounter in the education world: the conflict between implementing what we know works while running up
against what we know we can accomplish in the real world.

With that in mind, let me give you some insight into what
type of environment we have in Pennsylvania. One of the
great things about our country is that each state has its own
educational geography and territory. Pennsylvania is a large
state and locally controlled; we have 501 school districts. In
1999, we spent $16 billion on K–12 education—that's 44
percent of the state's total appropriations. It is also important to note that we are a strong union state. We have some
of the top compensation packages for teachers in the entire
country.

In that context, Governor Tom Ridge has made teacher
preparation and accountability a centerpiece of his education agenda. But that is on the microlevel. On the
macrolevel, what we have attempted to do is this: to get, in
a system that is and always has been downright resistant to
it, accurate and reliable indicators of performance and accountability. How do you achieve an educational bottom
line, as I like to call it, not only for the practitioners of education, the teachers and the education establishment, but
also for the clients of education?

The clients are the parents, the taxpayers, and the school
board members. Our job is to pass on information to them
that is accessible so that they can know how the schools are
performing, indeed, so they can reclaim ownership of them.
How do we judge how schools are performing? Well, it's exactly what you have been talking about this morning—we
must measure student performance.

Let me take this opportunity to discuss with you a bill that
our legislature recently passed and that Governor Ridge
signed into law in May 2000. It's called the Educational Empowerment Act. Twenty-two other states have similar laws
under which the state can go in and take over low-performing
school districts. But our program is a little bit different. Under
the Educational Empowerment Act, there are currently eleven

districts across Pennsylvania that qualify for state help. These eleven districts, including Philadelphia, the nation's fifth-largest district, all have 50 percent or more of their students flunking the state's assessment tests. Indeed, in some of these districts, 75 percent of fifth-graders are not passing state tests.

The help we have for these low-performing districts is twofold. First, we provide them with added flexibility. Districts can elect to contract out certain services to private firms, create more choice, reconstitute schools, or charter the entire district. Second, low-performing districts are eligible for additional resources, but it's very important to remember that most low-performing districts already spend well above state averages. This more flexible approach helps get at performance and results. If the district continues to falter, then the state will take over. The message is clear: districts are held accountable for student performance, they are given more flexibility to boost achievement, and they must suffer the consequences if they fall short.

Such an approach has also garnered support from across the aisle. Not only has the Ridge administration signed on to the plan, but several African-American, Democratic legislators from urban communities like Philadelphia also support the bill. The problems of urban education offer us the opportunity to build bipartisan coalitions to ensure that poor children in bad schools are given a chance at success. Nevertheless, the education establishment has been less than enthusiastic. The teacher unions opposed us, and when we confronted them they explained that although they, too, wanted to improve student performance, ultimately they were opposed to the proposal because it threatened job security for their members and allowed the districts too much control over hiring and firing teachers.

Another important development in Pennsylvania includes some of the recent action taken by the state board of education. In our state, the governor selects some members of the board, while others are appointed by the legislature. In a unanimous vote, the board recently approved a set of new teacher-preparation standards for Pennsylvania's more than ninety teacher-preparation programs.

The new standards focus on five main reforms. First, teachers must now take the same courses that are required for a major in the subject they plan to teach. Previously, prospective math teachers did not need to take the same courses as math majors; instead, they could major in education, math education, or some similar discipline. Now, new teachers must gain expertise in the rigors of their subject. Second, to enter a teacher-preparation program, students must have a B average in all of their college work up to the end of the first semester of their sophomore year. Third, while in the program, all students must maintain at least a B average to graduate. These are blunt instruments. From my career as a professor, I can tell you grades were not always a perfect indicator, but they are the best measure we have, and they're what we use.

Fourth, the board raised cut-off scores for certification examinations while also trying to improve the quality of the exams. When we first came to office, it was possible for teachers to score in the bottom deciles of these tests and still receive their certificates. For example, one question on the General Knowledge Test asked teachers to put in chronological order the New Deal, the Great Society, the Korean War, and World War II. People missed this question and still qualified to teach. We've tried to shore up the standards here.

Fifth, while Pennsylvania has an oversupply of certified teachers, the board recognized that we do not have an oversupply of qualified teachers. As such, the board has approved more alternative certification programs, which allow qualified professionals from other fields to transfer into teaching and avoid the hassles of going through the time-consuming traditional process. Also, Pennsylvania teachers obtain tenure after just three years and many stay in one school for their entire career, spanning twenty to thirty years. Before the board's action, there was no requirement for ongoing, rigorous professional development and teachers did not have to prove their skills on an ongoing basis. The board now requires teachers to be recertified every five years, which means all teachers periodically must go through professional development and be evaluated by their peers.

As I mentioned earlier, these are indeed blunt instruments, and they only get at the margins of what we discussed this morning, but at least we in Pennsylvania can now argue that we are making progress to improve the quality of teaching in our schools while also acknowledging that the teaching profession needs to be better. Let me also say that we are causing some anxiety in the teaching ranks.

The deans of the various schools of education in our state are not supportive of these reforms. The deans have consistently remained opposed to higher standards for the quality of their schools and the teachers who graduate from them. One dean said to me, "You know, grades don't matter, compassion matters." Although compassion is certainly an important attribute, can you imagine a dean saying that grades don't matter? Well, many in the education establishment feel that way. One of the members of our board of education who, to her credit, voted for our reform package once said to me, "I'll care what they know when I know that they care."

These statements highlight a very important divide in education. On the one hand, you have what the people—the parents and the taxpayers—want from their schools, and on the other, you have the teachers who think they already know what the people need. This is a huge disconnect that groups like Public Agenda have picked up on. The public wants teachers who can demonstrate knowledge, who can discipline a classroom, who can effectively manage a classroom. Indeed, the public consistently has wanted these things. But the schools of education want teachers who are able to show compassion, empathy, and caring. Again, these are worthy virtues, but citizens rightfully expect and demand accountability and performance. This is, after all, the backbone of the standards-based movement that has swept the nation in recent years. These desires are up against an establishment that tells the public to get beyond grades. According to them, teachers are there to mentor and nurture.

We have also made progress on other fronts in Pennsylvania. One of the key aspects of formulating public policy is the role of incentives. They are vital in policy making because incentives get people to do things they otherwise would not. Unfortunately, incentives really haven't played much of a role in education. We're trying to change that. We created a reform package in Pennsylvania that tells districts if they design an incentive program that rewards teachers for improving student performance, the state will help pay for it. It's important to note that we don't tell the district how to devise these incentive plans. Instead, the package forces district bargaining units to sit down and come up with a suitable plan that in some way ties teacher pay to how well students are performing. We think this is pretty much common sense. If districts are willing to take these steps that haven't been taken before, we're willing to help them pay for it.

Another point that I touched on earlier is professional development. We've really tried to reform these programs dramatically. We spend $100 million annually on professional development, and we must learn what works and what does not and spend wisely. We now have Governor's Schools for teachers, just like for students, where they can receive graduate credit. To ensure content and quality, we control the curriculum and staffing of these institutes. Previously, professional development was carried out by teachers' organizations and there was no quality control. We think that should be a requirement, and we've taken steps to reach that goal.

We also pretest and posttest our teachers when they go through professional development programs to see where they start and finish and to assess which of our programs work and which do not, again so we can spend wisely. Teacher testing is admittedly very controversial, but I believe it's a necessary step. I am in the process of developing more diagnostics for our professional development programs to ensure that they are getting the job done and that teachers are learning necessary skills.

Part of this also entails identifying best practices in teaching so that parents can know which philosophies are effective and which are not. Again, it is imperative that we make this information accessible to parents, the clients of education, so that they once again can have confidence in the schools. We have also gone to great lengths to expand the number of charter schools. These schools employ teachers who are open to reform and change and are willing to experiment with incentives and other reforms that have been resisted in traditional public schools. We are also implementing performance assessments for our teachers, based on their intellectual depth and accomplishments, not on years of service or pedagogy. This is yet another way of not just measuring inputs—we do a lot of that in education—but also assessing the impact teachers have on student performance and the results of their work.

That is also why we have hired Standard and Poors to assess every district's performance as a function of spending. As I mentioned earlier, in Pennsylvania, we spend a lot of money on our schools, and that's fine. But we have to know where our money is going and if it is being spent effectively. Standard and Poors will use a wide range of data and present reams of information to the public on just what their schools spend money on and what the impact is. Most important, they will establish objective, neutral benchmarks of performance. If student performance is better in one district than another, and at half the cost, then citizens and taxpayers need to know why.

Indeed, I'd like to return to what we've already discussed today. The impact teachers have on student performance is critical. As I said, it's one of the defining issues in education reform today. Yet traditionally we've ignored it and haven't valued it. The bottom line ought to be whether teaching improves student performance, not whether it leaves teachers feeling better about themselves. That's one of my problems with national certification of teachers. With that program, there is no link to student performance. Teachers who have received national certification often comment that the program makes them appreciate the profession more or that it motivates and inspires them in some way to be better teachers. Yet where's the evidence, where's the bottom line? There doesn't appear to be one.

I'd like to close on why teachers occupy a unique place in our democracy. Teachers often like to compare themselves with doctors, lawyers, and other professionals. Indeed, teaching requires a great deal of skill and education. Teachers have even developed their own mores, literature, and ethos, much of which is very difficult for the outside world to understand. Yet think about it: aren't teachers fundamentally different from these other professions?

We trust lawyers and doctors in specific areas because they have expertise we lack, because their expertise allows them to perform tasks we cannot. Their professional literature and practices are supposed to reflect this expertise and allow them to improve their skills.

Teachers are different. Their first and foremost obligation in a democracy is to effectively communicate with citizens, not just with themselves. We have confidence in teachers because the results of their labor are identified in our children, not because of their degrees or credentials. Citizens' confidence in a teacher's ability to improve student performance matters most. If we can move in that direction, the profession is better off.

Teacher Training and Pedagogical Methods

J. E. Stone

Recent studies have made it clear that significant differences in ability to improve student achievement exist among fully trained and experienced teachers. J. E. Stone's paper argues that these differences reflect the education community's view that student achievement is not public education's highest priority. Rather, achievement is only one valued outcome among many, and it often suffers from inattention.

The education community's priorities are consistent with ideals that have been taught in teacher training programs for decades, but especially since the sixties. They have come to constitute a pedagogical orthodoxy that the vast majority of educators treat as unquestionable.

The pedagogical concepts in which teachers are indoctrinated shape the education community's preference for schooling that is relatively ineffective and inefficient. Teachers are taught that it is more important to use stimulating and engaging practices than to use effective ones.

Teacher training and pedagogy is a topic that has not attracted the attention it deserves—at least until recently. Now—because of studies like that of June Rivers[1]—it is becoming clear that despite all the teacher training, credentialing, and annual evaluations that teachers have undergone for

---

[1]June C. Rivers-Sanders, "The Impact of Teacher Effect on Student Math Competency Achievement" (Ed.D. diss., University of Tennessee, 1999).

years, there are enormous differences in effectiveness among fully qualified and experienced teachers. I am going to discuss teacher training's contribution to teacher effectiveness.

OVERVIEW

The best research brings to mind several questions that we should ask about teacher training:

- Why is there so much variability in the effectiveness among fully trained and experienced teachers? All are trained and experienced, and all undergo regular in-service training.
- Why haven't the schools of education taken an interest in the success of public schools such as the "No Excuses" schools identified by Samuel Casey Carter and the Heritage Foundation? These are remarkably successful high-poverty schools, so they must have something to teach professional educators about teaching. The conventional wisdom is that teaching cannot overcome the effects of poverty.
- Why is value-added assessment not being studied and taught in schools of education, especially in areas where value-added data is used for school accountability? For example, Tennessee has had value-added assessment for eight years, and the Tennessee schools of education are ignoring it. None offers courses or workshops in it. Surely such a tool would be valuable to educators who are seeking the best ways to improve achievement.
- Why isn't the massive and unique value-added database being used for research by schools of education from all over the United States? If teacher educators are trying to find which types of teacher training work best, a database containing the value-added gains produced by graduates of various teacher-training programs would be a gold mine of information.

In my opinion, the answer to all of these questions is disquieting but clear: the schools of education are not really interested in teaching that is primarily intended to improve achievement. In fact, they disapprove of such teaching. They frown on it because they disagree with the proposition that student achievement is the most important outcome of schooling, that is, that student achievement is the indispensable outcome. In their view, schooling that fails to produce achievement is not necessarily failed schooling.

I am going to try to show you why they have this view.

BACKGROUND

Before I begin discussing teacher training quality, there are some things you should know about my background and my perspective. I am licensed as an educational psychologist and a school psychologist, and I am a professor in a school of education. I was trained in educational psychology at the University of Florida, Gainesville, and I have taught graduate and undergraduate courses in child, developmental, and educational psychology at East Tennessee for nearly thirty years.

My experience has mainly been in the front lines of teacher training. In the early nineties, however, I encountered a situation that strongly influenced my thinking about the need for teacher-training reform. The high school attended by my two sons decided to become a leader in educational innovation. I won't spend time telling you about their proposed innovations. I will say that something like 85 percent of the parents—including me—were opposed, but despite anything we could say or do, the school's plans were implemented.

That experience permitted me to see in a very personal way how schools treat outside influences and how the doctrines that prevail within the education community place it at odds with what most parents want, indeed with what most of the larger public wants. In 1995, it led me to found the Education Consumers ClearingHouse—a company that provides public education's consumers with access to consumer-friendly networking, information, and expertise.

Although I am an education professor, I have a consumer's perspective—and that makes a difference. The views of education's consumers are not necessarily agreeable to education's providers. The schools typically think of parents as the junior partners in the school-home relationship. To the contrary, ClearingHouse subscribers generally believe that schools—like hospitals—should offer advice but otherwise respect the aims of parents whether they agree or not.

CONSUMER AIMS VERSUS EDUCATOR AIMS

A recent initiative of the ClearingHouse has been the formation of an Education Consumers Consultants Network—a group of educators and professors like myself who provide consumer-friendly expertise to parent organizations, school board members, legislators, and others on the consumer side of the education marketplace.

Recently, three members of our consultants' network—a professor at the University of Louisville, another at Western Washington University, and I—have been working on what we call a "Second Opinion." A consumer group in a Western state asked us to render an opinion with regard to a series of policies and legislative enactments that are being undertaken to reform teacher training in that state. Our objective has been to decipher the blizzard of information put out by the various organizations and agencies and to assess how well these plans and activities are likely to serve the interests and objectives of the consuming public.

As part of this project, I reviewed newspaper accounts of the various events, and I noticed a pattern. Events that drew positive comments from educators were often not well received by noneducators. The opposite was true, too. Events that were welcomed by noneducators were often not well received by educators.

I don't mean to belabor the point, but I find many of the differences in opinion that we hear in public conversations about schooling to be differences between consumers and providers.[2] Obviously there are overlaps, but producers seem to be primarily concerned about how schools operate, whereas consumers are primarily concerned about whether they are producing expected benefits, that is, concerns about process versus concerns about outcomes. What I want to discuss is what these differences are, why they exist, and how they are related to teacher training.

Differing Educational Priorities

The differences between consumers and providers go beyond factors such as professional expertise and familiarity with schoolhouse life. They stem both from different concepts of education[3] and from practical considerations. The discussion that follows centers on conceptual differences, but, as you will no doubt surmise for yourself, there are social, political, and economic factors at work, too.

In a word, both consumers and educators want the best for children, but they have different ideas about what is important. Consumers want results. Educators agree, but they believe that policy makers should defer to the education community's judgment in defining the result and setting the process by which it is measured.

Public education's consumers believe that schools should teach children the knowledge and skills that parents and taxpayers consider essential for happy, responsible, and productive lives.[4] Through their elected representatives, the public establishes curricula; states

---

[2]"Reality Check 2000"—an annual survey conducted by Public Agenda and published by *Education Week* 19, no. 23 (February 16, 2000): S1–S8—reported marked differences between the views of employers and college professors and those of teachers. Professors and employers were highly dissatisfied with the knowledge and skills of high school graduates. Teachers thought schools were already doing a better job than most people think.

[3]J. Stone, "Aligning Teacher Training with Public Policy," *The State Education Standard* 1, no. 1 (Winter 2000).

[4]J. Johnson and J. Immerwahr, *First Things First: What Americans Expect from the Public Schools* (New York: Public Agenda, 1994).

course and grade-level objectives; sets policies regarding report cards, standardized tests, and so on; and otherwise acts to ensure that students will learn that which their parents and other members of the community expect them to learn. Education's consumers believe that effective schools and effective teachers are those that are successful in bringing about prescribed results and that true educational reform should serve to improve these results.

Teachers, professors of education, educators who work for the state education agencies, and other members of the education community, that is, public education's providers, generally take a different view. They believe that the knowledge and skills that consumers consider important are only one part of a broad range of considerations with which schools and teachers must concern themselves. They value academic achievement, but not necessarily as a top priority. They believe that children have varied needs and that ideally schooling should be accommodated to those differences in a way that optimizes overall educational growth—they are concerned with the "whole child."[5]

Education's providers hold as ideal those teaching methodologies that are intended to guide or encourage or facilitate "educational growth" in ways that are sensitive to student differences.[6] They denigrate and oppose the use of those methods that prescribe, expect, or require unaccustomed levels of student effort and accomplishment. They favor flexible curricula, narrative report cards, portfolio assessment, and teacher autonomy. They resist prescriptive curricula, letter grades, standardized tests, and teacher ac-

---

[5]For an engaging account of the rise and fall of a school embodying all that is currently considered "best practice," see D. Frantz and C. Collins, *Celebration USA* (New York: Henry Holt and Company, 1999). "Celebration" is the name of the model school developed by Walt Disney World.

[6]S. Zemelman, H. Daniels, and A. Hyde, *Best Practice: New Standards for Teaching and Learning in America's Schools* (Portsmouth, N.H.: Heineman Publishers, 1988).

countability.[7] They believe that good schools and good teachers are those that maximize stimulation and opportunities for student enrichment, and they think of educational improvement as growth in the availability of enriching educational experiences.

By the way, the perspective I am describing is in education's mainstream. There are educators whose views lean more toward schooling as an instrument of social and economic reform, and their views are in much greater disagreement with the public than the ones I am describing.[8]

Both education's consumers and education's providers talk about learning and achievement, but they accord it very different priorities.[9] Educators believe that using correct pedagogical process is more important than attaining any particular level of mastery. Their reason for valuing process over outcome is that they believe optimal educational outcomes—that is, a kind of balanced growth of the whole—are possible only when the right kind of teaching is used. They refer to such teaching as "best practice."

Best practice teaching is the open-ended, facilitative, guide-on-the-side type of teaching that is extolled by professors of education.[10] It is also called learner-centered instruction because it theoretically puts the overall interests of the learner first—in other words, ahead of the teacher's interest in the student's acquisition of knowledge and skills. In the world of teacher education, learner-centered instruction is the standard against which all other forms of teaching are judged.

In theory, learner-centered instruction permits the student to grow in a way that respects the full range of individual

---

[7]Public Agenda, "Reality Check 2000."

[8]See T. Jennings, "Developmental Psychology and the Preparation of Teachers Who Affirm Diversity: Strategies Promoting Critical Social Consciousness in Teacher Preparation Programs," *Journal of Teacher Education* 46, no. 4 (1995).

[9]For a revealing look at the aims and views of teacher educators, see G. Farkas, J. Johnson, and A. Duffett, *Different Drummers: How Teachers of Teachers View Public Education* (New York: Public Agenda, 1997).

[10]Zemelman, Daniels, and Hyde, *Best Practice.*

needs, not simply in ways that parents or teachers believe important. Instruction fitted to individual student needs is believed to be conducive to the emergence of a personal synthesis of understanding, that is, an understanding that is practical, not abstract and bookish, relevant to the learner's life, and fully integrated into the individual's worldview. For example, in *constructivism*—a popular learner-centered view—the desired outcome of an educational experience is for the learner to construct personal meaning.

Learner-centered instruction is intended to be naturalistic— the sort of learning that takes place when experience is the teacher. When experience teaches, however, one never knows whether that which was taught is that which was learned; and to education's consumers, uncertain outcomes are a problem. They believe that certain types of knowledge and skills must be attained for an individual to become a productive and responsible member of society. They also believe that schools should urge students to maximize their talents.

These are subtle but enormously significant differences. Learner-centered instruction is not simply an alternative means of arriving at the objectives sought by parents and policy makers. It is an approach that places a distinctly lower value on students knowing and understanding the accumulated wisdom of past generations. Instead, it emphasizes individuals forming their own ideas and assessing the worth of these insights from their immediate life experiences, that is, from the school of hard knocks. It is an approach that claims to equip students with thinking skills instead of knowledge. The public, by contrast, disagrees that thinking skills are sufficient even if it were possible to produce them in isolation.

I could go further in discussing the various ways in which the education community's ideal process is at odds with consumer expectations, but an example might be more helpful. Think of teaching tennis or golf. You could introduce children to either sport by just giving them a club or racquet and letting them have at it. Or you could start them with lessons in the basics. The former is more or less the approach that the education community idealizes, and the latter is more or less what the public wants.

Kids might find the unstructured approach more fun and might consider the organized lessons boring, but few parents would be willing to pay for discovery-based golf or tennis instruction—and neither would taxpayers. Yet that is the ideal taught to most teachers.

More to the point, boring or not, starting with the basics is a far more certain means of producing skilled golfers and tennis players, and, plainly, that is the premier consideration with regard to basic skills like reading, writing, and arithmetic. Kids can live without golf or tennis skills, but they can't do without sound academics. That's why parents want teachers to teach rather than just facilitate and hope for the best. Responsible adults understand what school success or failure means to a child's future, so they want children to learn certain things and they want those things learned to the best of the child's ability. Schooling is valuable precisely because it equips children with knowledge and skills that they do not yet recognize as important. Yes, most will figure it out on their own when they are thirty-five, but that is exactly the kind of trauma that loving parents want their children to avoid.

HOW PEDAGOGICAL DOCTRINE INFLUENCES SCHOOL EFFECTIVENESS

As a practical matter, educators recognize that not all students respond well to learner-centered instruction, and they have an explanation: not all students are "ready to learn." They believe students fail to respond properly because their life circumstances have not adequately prepared them and/or because there is some mismatch between the student's unique characteristics and the opportunities afforded by the school. In principle, at least, if society can give proper support and if schools can respond properly to their unique characteristics, the talents, interests, and energies of each student will be freed for intellectual pursuits. In other words, "all students can learn," that is, all students can benefit from "best practice" teaching.[11]

Although described in a variety of ways, this concept of teaching's relationship to learning has been a staple of mainstream pedagogy since the early years of the twentieth century. It was the foundation of the child-centered teaching of the twenties and the progressive education of the thirties and forties. It originated as an appealing alternative to the often-regimented classrooms of the late 1800s, and it has stood as an unquestioned norm ever since.[12] In theory, teachers trained in "enlightened" classroom methods would be helpful and sympathetic mentors, not taskmasters with a hickory stick. It was a concept that greatly bolstered public acceptance of the idea that teachers need specialized training, not mere subject matter expertise. It began as the "learning can be fun" approach, and it has become the "learning must be fun" approach.

Fitting Instruction to Diversity

Over the last thirty or forty years, learner-centered methods have attempted to individualize instruction to a variety of cognitive, developmental, socioeconomic, cultural, racial, and personality characteristics.[13] The study of student diversity has become the overweening passion of education professors; and teachers, of course, have been thoroughly indoctrinated with the idea that their first responsibility is to

---

[11]Ibid.

[12]E. D. Hirsch, *The Schools We Need and Why We Don't Have Them* (New York: Doubleday, 1996). "Within the education community, there is currently no *thinkable* (Hirsch's italics) alternative" (69); ". . . the heretical suggestion that the creed itself might be faulty cannot be uttered. To question progressive doctrine would be to put in doubt the identity of the education profession itself" (69).

[13]See L. Darling-Hammond, G. Griffin, and A. Wise, *Excellence in Teacher Education: Helping Teachers Develop Learner-Centered Schools*, ed. R. McClure (Washington, D.C.: National Education Association, 1992). The widespread support enjoyed by learner-centered schooling is evidenced by its recognition among well-known educational leaders. Drs. Darling-Hammond and Wise are the directors of the National Commission on Teaching and America's Future and the National Council for the Accreditation of Teacher Education, respectively.

be aware of and sensitive to such differences in their curricular and instructional planning.

There are mountains of research on the identification of student differences and an equally large number of studies showing degrees of relationship between student characteristics and success in school. However, what is lacking in most cases is any convincing evidence that teachers can fine-tune instruction to these differences in such a way as to produce significant improvements in measured achievement. In fact, the entire vein of educational research called "attribute-treatment interaction studies" is generally conceded to have been a failure.[14] What teachers are told, however, is that student differences are important and that if their teaching is truly creative, energetic, and engaging, they will succeed in individualizing and bringing forth the best from all students. In effect, teachers are being taught to make diagnoses that heighten their awareness of differences without advancing their ability to teach.

Attention to diversity may not have made teachers more effective, but it has influenced their ideas about how schooling should be improved. If individualization is necessary to learning, lower pupil-teacher ratios and the use of specialized personnel are the key prerequisites to any real improvement. Conceptually, more personnel permit greater differentiation of services and therefore a better fit for each student. Educators say to parents: "Does your child have different developmental needs? Then he or she needs a teacher specially trained to work with those needs." "Your child has different talents? Then your child needs a teacher trained to maximize those talents." "Your child is racially or culturally different? Then your child needs a teacher who can fit his or her teaching to those differences."

One impact of this thinking as it has been applied over the last century has been an incredible expansion and diversification of school staffing. If there is an identifiable uniqueness

---

[14]See R. Snow and J. Swanson, "Instructional Psychology: Aptitude, Adaptation, and Assessment," *Annual Review of Psychology* 43 (1992): 583–626.

(and a supportive constituency), the education community will create a specialty that is said to be skilled in maximizing the educational growth of such students. School personnel now include not only a variety of subject matter specialists but also teachers trained specifically for middle schools, primary schools, kindergartens, and preschools. In addition, there are arts, music, and physical education teachers as well as trained counselors, psychologists, nurses, social workers, and a huge variety of special educators, all overseen by layer upon layer of supervisory and administrative personnel.

EFFECTIVENESS AND COST

As Eric Hanushek points out, the academic gains garnered by adding personnel and lowering class size have been small and costly relative to other means of increasing achievement. For example, far greater gains are attainable—and at much lower cost—using proven, result-oriented teaching methods. However, educators rarely adopt result-oriented methods, much less experimentally proven methods because virtually all such methods disagree with the learner-centered, whole-child, balanced-outcomes ideals promulgated by the schools of education.[15]

Instead of seeking to accommodate to student differences, result-oriented methods seek first to bring about learning. If accommodating to a particular uniqueness—entry-level knowledge and skill, for example—is known to produce improvement in learning, result-oriented methods acknowledge and make use of them. Otherwise, they ignore them.

Teachers are taught that any methodology that ignores learner-centered ideals is, in effect, a step toward the return of the hickory stick. They are given to believe that any deviation from methodology intended to address the growth of the "whole child" is a risky scheme. Of course, such claims

---

[15]A recent discussion of the issue is D. Carnine, *Why Education Experts Resist Effective Practices* (April 2000). Available at the Thomas B. Fordham Foundation Web site, *www.edexcellence.net*.

are founded on belief, not research, but they have a profound impact on the kind of practices teachers favor and the kind they avoid. Instead of looking for the most stimulating and engaging methods among those that are known to be effective, teachers are taught to do the reverse. They look among the fun methods and try to find ones that produce results. The outcome, of course, is the sort of "edutainment" that is commonly found in today's public school classrooms. These lessons may look very stimulating and appealing, but they produce little in the way of substantive results.

A prime example of an effective teaching methodology rejected on the grounds that it conflicts with pedagogical doctrine is Direct Instruction (DI), which is a highly structured approach with scripted lesson plans. DI is as thoroughly tested and proven a teaching methodology as has ever been developed, and it has been around for thirty years. In Project Follow Through—one of the largest educational experiments ever conducted—not only was Direct Instruction the most effective, but it also did the best job of boosting student self-esteem, the personal growth that teacher educators claim will be undermined by an overemphasis on achievement.[16] Teachers, nonetheless, have ignored and rejected DI because it deviates from the learner-centered ideal. Despite an absence of credible negative evidence, they suspect that it has an adverse effect on student and teacher creativity.[17]

In matters of pedagogical effectiveness, evidence has little impact because teachers are inundated with learner-centered propaganda.[18] For example, anyone reading the curricular

---

[16]C. L. Watkins, "Project Follow Through: A Story of the Identification and Neglect of Effective Instruction," *Youth Policy* (July 1988): 7–11.

[17]Carnine, "Why Education Experts Resist."

[18]See J. E. Johnson and K. M. Johnson, "Clarifying the Developmental Perspective in Response to Carta, Schwartz, Atwater, and McConnell," *Topics in Early Childhood Special Education* 12, no. 4 (1992): 439–457. The authors write about a committee meeting they attended at one of the formative gatherings of the National Association for Early Childhood Education. They describe how the pedagogical term "developmentally appropriate instruction" was adopted as a concept that might be used for public relations purposes.

guidelines of an organization like the National Association for the Education of Young Children (NAEYC) would suppose that one of the greatest risks to the educational well-being of American children is academic burn-out resulting from premature attempts to teach the ABCs, teaching children before they were "developmentally ready." Of course, the opposite is true. The greatest hazard to the educational well-being of American children is the *failure* of schools to teach them basics such as the ABCs. What the NAEYC and so many other educators fail to consider is that whatever the suspected risk from overzealous teaching, it must be balanced against the enormous and well-documented risk of failing to teach.

CURRENT REFORMS IN TEACHER EDUCATION

Forgive me if I seem to have gone overboard in discussing the thinking that prevails in schools of education, but I believe that the critical issue in understanding teacher training's relationship to teacher effectiveness is the one of correctly framing the problem. What I have tried to show you is that *the core problem is one of wrongheaded training,* that is, training in pedagogy that treats measured student achievement as an incidental outcome of some ideal form of pedagogical practice in which the teacher education community's notions about ideal process are considered more important than the consuming public's desire for improved student achievement.

For decades, members of the lay public and lay policy makers have prodded, encouraged, and supported the education community's efforts at improvement. What they have gotten in return is a seemingly unending cycle of innovations, fads, failures, and reforms, most of which have been variants or refinements of pedagogical ideals that have been around since the early part of the last century. *These "improvements" are coming right out of the schools of education, and they are creating problems, not merely failing to solve them.*

Taxpayers are spending zillions on educational reforms that have been necessitated by the faulty and ineffective practices in which teachers have been trained. The self-esteem-boosting fad of the sixties and seventies is an excellent example. Proponents believed that students fail to benefit from schooling because they lack positive self-regard. In many schools of education, teachers were taught that the student's need for self-esteem must be fulfilled before study, learning, and achievement can be expected. Whole courses were dedicated to teaching teachers how to facilitate the growth of self-esteem. Self-esteem improvement became so thoroughly ingrained in teaching that, at one point, U.S. students may have been world leaders in self-esteem despite their abysmal academic performance.

As is the case with class-size reduction, there was research showing a modest relationship between high levels of self-esteem and academic achievement. As it turns out, however, self-esteem was related to school success not because high self-esteem is necessary to learning but because academic success elevates self-esteem. In other words, the self-esteem researchers had it backward. Improved self-esteem is a by-product of educational success, not a cause of it.

One of the programs tested in the above-noted Follow Through Project of the sixties and seventies—the Open Education model—employed self-esteem boosting as its principal intervention. The students taught by this method did *significantly worse* on both basic academic skills and cognitive skills as a result of their participation.

To my knowledge, the cost of this and other mistaken ideas has never been calculated. Neither have costs of any other of the many, many ideas that schools of education have propagated without any credible evidence that they work. We could spend days cataloging them.

Think of what California alone is having to spend trying to retrain teachers trained in whole language. Look at the social and political costs of trying to change the sincere but ill-founded beliefs now held by a generation of teachers. Think of the numbers of students and citizens who may never be able to read proficiently. Forget the costs to the taxpayers. Just look at the diminished prospects of the children who were the subjects of this experiment.

The NCTAF Initiative

Now let's look at the current efforts to improve teacher training. Will they prevent the reemergence of nonsense like self-esteem boosting? Will they ensure that teachers are able to recognize the value of teaching models such as Direct Instruction? Will they require pedagogical enthusiasms such as whole language to be proven before they are disseminated? In my opinion, the answer is clearly "no." They are reforms instituted by the same organizational and institutional stakeholders who have led teacher training all along. They are reforms embodying the same pedagogical doctrines that have underpinned teacher training for at least the last fifty years.

The principal efforts to reform teacher training are being led by the National Commission on Teaching and America's Future (NCTAF).[19] The NCTAF is aggressively urging policy makers at the state level to adopt the training standards set by the National Council for the Accreditation of Teacher Education (NCATE); the teacher licensure standards set by the Interstate New Teacher Assessment and Support Consortium (INTASC, a group working under the auspices of the Council of Chief State School Officers); and the advanced teacher certification standards set by the National Board of Professional Teaching Standards (NBPTS).

This entire initiative is premised on the idea that the chief problems affecting teacher quality are insufficient numbers of fully trained teachers, insufficient training for teachers, insufficient regulation, and inadequate standards. I could not disagree more. In my view, it is obvious that whatever short-

---

[19]See M. Kanstoroom and C. Finn, eds., *Better Teachers, Better Schools* (Washington, D.C.: Thomas B. Fordham Foundation, July 1999) for a discussion of the efforts being undertaken by the NCTAF, NCATE, INTASC, and NBPTS.

ages and inadequacies may exist, they pale in comparison to the problems of misdirected training, misdirected regulation, and mismatched standards.

Instead of training teachers to improve student achievement, current teacher-training programs—including those that are NCATE-approved—are indoctrinating them in pedagogical concepts that embody educational priorities at odds with those of the consuming and taxpaying public. Adoption of the NCTAF proposals may improve teacher quality as conceived by the teacher education community, but if anything, it will make matters worse for education's consumers. Teachers not indoctrinated in learner-centered views will become harder to find.

I want to be clear about my message. I am not saying that members and staff of the NCTAF and all the many individuals who are working in concert with them are not genuinely trying to improve teacher quality. My point is that these changes have little to do with advancing what most parents and taxpayers want. The NCTAF is mainly composed of representatives of the education community. That they subscribe to the principles that have guided the education community for years is not surprising. The NCTAF has reams of research supporting its proposals, but virtually all are studies that define teacher quality in ways consistent with the education community's aims, not with those of the public. The NCTAF-inspired reforms are one more attempt to improve teacher training by promoting the wider use of pedagogical practices that have failed for generations.

WHY VALUE-ADDED ASSESSMENT OF TEACHER EFFECTIVENESS COULD MAKE A SIGNIFICANT DIFFERENCE

The NCTAF's strategy is to improve teacher quality through closer scrutiny of teacher competencies—a strategy with which I certainly agree. They propose to look at both subject matter knowledge and pedagogical expertise. The concept of testing teachers for subject matter competence is sound because knowledge is a valid prerequisite to successful teaching and credible tests are available. As many have noted, teachers cannot teach what they don't know.

The assessment of pedagogical expertise, however, is another matter entirely. Policy makers and the public assume that tests such as the Praxis (formerly the National Teachers Examination) can measure a teacher's ability to bring about student achievement. In fact, they are not valid in that sense at all. Rather, they measure whether teachers have learned that which their professors taught them, which is the "best practices" favored by the schools of education. As was made clear by the recent report of the National Research Council's Committee on Assessment and Teacher Quality, "There is currently little evidence available about the extent to which widely used teacher licensure tests distinguish between candidates who are minimally competent to teach and those who are not." "[Teacher licensure tests] are not designed to predict who will become effective teachers."[20]

The same can be said about all of the various portfolios, rubrics, and classroom performance indicators that are embodied in the "competency-based" approaches to teacher assessment now recommended by the NCATE, the INTASC, and the NBPTS.[21] All afford the candidate the opportunity to exhibit his or her grasp of "pedagogically correct" methodology, not of practices that are known to bring about increases in measured achievement. From a consumer standpoint, these assessments

---

[20]Committee on Assessment and Teacher Quality, Board on Testing and Assessment, National Research Council, *Tests and Teaching Quality, Interim Report* (Washington, D.C.: National Academy Press, 2000).

[21]For details of the evaluative procedures and processes used by the NCATE, see National Council for the Accreditation of Teacher Education, *Program Standards for Elementary Teacher Preparation* (Washington, D.C.: National Council for the Accreditation of Teacher Education, 1999) and the just-released *NCATE 2000 Unit Standards* (Washington, D.C., 2000). The NBPTS uses portfolios and videotapes in their reviews of teachers seeking advanced certification, and its standards and principles are parallel to those of the NCATE. See National Board for Professional Teaching Standards, *What Every Teacher Should Know: The National Board Certification Process, 1998–1999* (Southfield, Mich.: National Board for Professional Teaching Standards, April 1998). The latest revisions of both NCATE and NBPTS standards are available at their respective Web sites.

are nothing more than a new way of ensuring that trained teachers are all grounded in the same ill-suited doctrines.[22]

Several recent reports agree that sound methods of assessing teacher quality are sorely needed. A 1999 U.S. Department of Education report concluded, ". . . indicators of teacher preparation and qualifications do not directly address the actual quality of instructional practices."[23] Similarly, an April 2000 report by the American Federation of Teachers called for teacher-training programs to develop a credible core curriculum in pedagogy: "We can no longer tolerate a 'do your own thing' pedagogy curriculum."[24] An improved exit/licensure test was one of its major recommendations. A fall 1999 report by the American Council on Education not only called for improved assessment of teachers but also bluntly urged college presidents to either strengthen the quality of teacher-training programs or close them.[25]

Tests of pedagogical knowledge and competency-based assessments of pedagogical skill are valid to the extent that they serve as proxies for effective teaching. In other words, they are valid to the extent that they predict what a teacher will actually do with students. The problem, however, is that the available tests and assessments have all been validated against the criterion of what *teachers and professors* think novice teachers should know and be able to do rather than

---

[22]A recent article suggests that candidates who are successful in meeting the certification standards set by the NBPTS must adopt "NBPTS discourse values, which may be at odds with teachers' 'working knowledge.'" See R. Burroughs, T. Roe, M. Hendricks-Lee, "Communities of Practice and Discourse Communities: Negotiating Boundaries in NBPTS Certification," *Teachers College Record* 102, no. 2 (2000): 2344–374.

[23]National Center for Education Statistics, *Teacher Quality: A Report on the Preparation and Qualifications of Public School Teachers* (Washington, D.C.: National Center for Education Statistics, January 1999).

[24]American Federation of Teachers, Report of the K-16 Teacher Education Task Force, *Building a Profession: Strengthening Teacher Preparation and Induction* (Washington, D.C.: American Federation of Teachers, April 2000).

[25]American Council on Education, *To Touch the Future: Report of the ACE Presidents' Task Force on Teacher Education* (Washington, D.C.: American Council on Education, 1999).

what *the public* wants them to know and be able to do. In other words, buried in the debate about teacher quality are competing definitions of quality. One is quality as defined by the NCTAF et al., and the other is quality as defined by the public and by value-added assessment.

Teacher Effectiveness Defined by the Public

Value-added assessment of a novice teacher's ability to bring about student achievement solves the problems of uncertainty and bias in the assessment of teacher competence by observing the criterion of teacher effectiveness instead of its fallible predictors. It defines teacher quality as the demonstrated ability to increase student achievement, the public's definition. With value-added assessment, policy makers would no longer be dependent on test scores and subjective interpretations that embody a hidden set of educational priorities. Instead, they would, in effect, stipulate the meaning of teacher effectiveness and teacher-training effectiveness in a way that is aligned with the public's educational priorities.[26]

Unlike training in law and medicine, teacher education has never had to respect consumer priorities because its graduates have never had to survive in a marketplace. Top-down regulation of teacher training has been largely ineffective, as well. The agencies in charge of regulating teacher education were originally formed to promote the expansion and enhancement of public education, not to perform oversight and control. They have been subject to what economists call "regulatory capture"—they are unduly influenced by the parties they are trying to regulate. The training, licensure, and certification standards now in place were all approved by state education agencies.

With value-added indicators of teacher effectiveness in place, policy makers would be able to identify successful

---

[26]Stone, "Aligning Teacher Training with Public Policy," 34–38.

programs and adjust their support accordingly. School officials would have a much improved basis for making hiring, tenure, and promotion decisions, and parents, of course, would be pleased to have assurance that their child's teachers were meeting objectively measured performance standards.

Teachers, perhaps more than anyone, would benefit from a change to objective assessment of their work. One of the most frustrating aspects of teaching is that you can do an excellent job of getting students to learn and your efforts may never be noticed, much less appreciated. Even if test scores are reviewed, they are subject to administrator interpretation; and teachers well understand that friendly administrators make friendly interpretations and unfriendly administrators make unfriendly ones. With value-added assessment, the results are visible and they speak for themselves.

Subjective job performance assessments flavored with favoritism are among the most demoralizing and demeaning aspects of teaching in public education. In the absence of objective performance data, it is no wonder that teachers prefer salary schedules based on time-in-grade and earned credentials. In Tennessee, where value-added assessments of teacher performance have been in place for some years, teachers are gradually being won over.[27]

Students seeking a career in teaching would also be able to make good use of value-added data. They would be able to see which schools of education were training effective teachers and which school systems were hiring them. Over time, teacher-training programs whose graduates get the good jobs would flourish and those whose graduates were less successful would decline.

---

[27]For a description of the Tennessee Value-Added Assessment System, its developer, Professor William Sanders, and its growth as a tool for assessing teacher performance, see D. Hill, "He's Got Your Number," *Teacher Magazine* 11, no. 8 (May 2000): 42–47.

Title II of the 1998 Higher Education Act required teacher-training programs to report on the quality of their graduates. One problem has been a lack of data comparable from one state to another. Teacher performance data, such as that now collected by Tennessee's Value-Added Assessment System, would be an excellent gauge of program performance, and it could be compiled in any state that has already been regularly gathering student achievement data.[28] Given the education community's aversion to standardized tests and its affinity for so-called authentic assessment, value-added assessment of achievement gains would seem to be an attractive alternative to the proposed exams of pedagogical knowledge.

Realistically, program assessments based on the value-added performance of novice teachers would have to be phased in over a period of several years. Substantial rethinking and curricular adjustment would be necessary. The change would not be easy, if for no other reason than shortages in appropriately trained faculty. However, with the growth of on-site training in local schools and similar alternatives, the need for trained teachers would be served by either reformed schools of education or their replacements.

---

[28]Hill, "He's Got Your Number." Also see J. Stone, "Value-Added Assessment: An Accountability Revolution," in Kanstoroom and Finn, eds., *Better Teachers, Better Schools.*

Teaching Methods

Herbert J. Walberg

In this piece, Dr. Herb Walberg documents effective teaching methods and examines which, if any, are implemented in classrooms in the United States. Walberg, an internationally respected education psychologist, is renowned for his work comparing elementary and primary education systems in different countries. In most instances, Walberg finds that American schools do not emphasize effective teaching methods and have failed to implement successful learning strategies used elsewhere.

Specifically, Walberg examines several factors, including the average amount of homework American teachers typically assign and how much time children spend in school in the United States. He finds that when compared with students in countries like China and Korea, American students spend about half as much time studying each year as their counterparts. Empirical evidence suggests that study time is positively related to student performance, and according to Walberg, this time factor is a major reason for American students' slipping further and further behind students in other countries.

Overall, Walberg lists several components, like clearly identified academic standards, direct teaching, and encouraging increased parental involvement, that when used together, improve learning. These strategies are hardly revolutionary; they are well-known and effective educational practices that have been used in other countries and in many high-performing schools in the United States. The real mystery is why they have not been implemented on a larger scale in a greater number of public schools. Until educators accept and implement these proven methods, the prospects for improved student outcomes remain bleak.

INTRODUCTION AND OVERVIEW

As an educational psychologist, I have had a thirty-five-year interest in identifying the methods and conditions within and outside classrooms that help improve student performance. Educators should choose those methods that positively, consistently, and powerfully affect how much children learn. To do this, they could turn to the hundreds of studies and thousands of comparisons concerning the relative effects of various educational conditions and methods. But this research literature is voluminous and scattered. So I have tried to synthesize the research in various publications, the most recent of which provide the sources for this chapter.[1]

The direct, immediate, powerful, consistent, and psychological causes of learning may be divided into the nine factors shown in Table 1 on page 57. My focus in this chapter is on instructional methods, but the table makes clear that student aptitude and psychological environments are also pervasive influences on learning. Children may learn little, for example, if they are unmotivated to learn or if in the 87 percent of their waking hours spent outside school in the first eighteen years of life they are not stimulated to develop their vocabulary and other academic ingredients of success. Still, teaching methods

---

[1]These include Herbert J. Walberg and Geneva D. Haertel, eds., *Psychology and Educational Practice* (Berkeley, Calif.: McCutchan Publishing, 1997); Hersholt C. Waxman and Herbert J. Walberg, eds., *New Directions for Teaching Research and Practice* (Berkeley, Calif.: McCutchan Publishing, 1999); Herbert J. Walberg, "Uncompetitive American Schools," in Diane Ravitch, ed., *Brookings Papers on Education Policy* (Washington, D.C.: Brookings Institution, 1999); Arthur J. Reynolds and Herbert J. Walberg, eds., *Evaluation Research for Educational Productivity* 7 (Greenwich, Conn.: JAI Press, 1998); Herbert J. Walberg and Jin-Shei Lai, "Meta-Analytic Effects for Policy," in Gregory J. Cizek, ed., *Handbook of Educational Policy* (San Diego, Calif.: Academic Press, 1999); and Herbert J. Walberg, "Generic Methods," in Gordon Cawelti, ed., *Handbook on Improving Student Achievement* (Alexandria, Va.: Educational Research Service, 1998).

TABLE 1   Nine Educational Productivity Factors

A. Student aptitude
  1. Ability or prior achievement
  2. Development as indexed by chronological age or stage of maturation
  3. Motivation or self-concept as indicated by personality tests or the student's willingness to persevere intensively on learning tasks
B. Teaching methods
  1. Amount of time students engage in learning
  2. Quality of the instructional learning experience, including
    a. Organization of subject matter
    b. Pedagogy or psychological principles of teaching
C. Psychological environments
  1. "Curriculum of the home"
  2. Morale or student perception of classroom social group
  3. Peer group outside school
  4. Minimal leisure-time television viewing

---

should be of great interest, since, of the nine factors, they are most alterable by educators and policy makers.

This main body of this chapter is divided into four sections. The next three sections divide teaching methods into three aspects corresponding to Table 1, namely, the amount the child is taught, the organization of the subject matter, and the pedagogical techniques. The fourth section treats the context or conditions of teaching.

AMOUNT OF TEACHING

My compilation of 376 estimates of the effect of the amount of teaching and assigned and voluntary study time on children's learning revealed that 88 percent were positive.[2] This may be

---

[2]See Walberg, "Meta-Analytic Effects for Policy."

the most consistent finding of all psychological research on academic learning, but the obvious conclusion may not even require such documentation.

Yet the policy implication has hardly been implemented in the United States, which still has one of the shortest school years among rich countries and whose children do less homework than their counterparts in advanced Asian and European countries. Two of my students have examined study habits of Chinese and Korean students. Since the Asian students have more days in their school year and more homework and often attend after-school tutoring schools, it appears that they have about twice the total annual study time of American students. The time factor is a major reason for U.S. children falling further and further behind during the school year.

Studies of how American children spend their time show that they would lose little in order to study more, since television and other non–educationally productive, passive, sedentary, and even harmful activities consume much of their outside-school time. There are, however, some encouraging examples: Chicago public schools give underperforming students a choice of repeating a grade or trying to catch up in summer school. Many Asian families who have recently immigrated to the United States send their children to private tutoring schools. I sit on the board of the privately supported Academic Development Institute in Chicago, which provides programs for parents to stimulate their children's academic progress at home and at school through leisure reading, learning about their children's academic strengths and weaknesses, taking their children to museums, and the like.

Nevertheless, the root causes of American students' poor study habits are the short school year of 180 days originating in our agrarian society of long ago, our lack of rigorous academic standards, and the failure of school boards, educators, and parents to insist on a larger amount of serious academic work, including homework.

CURRICULUM CONTENT ORGANIZATION

Curriculum is a vast field that can be treated at encyclopedic length. My focus is not on what to teach but on how the subject may be best organized. Specifically, my focus is on our distinctive American problem—the lack of uniform content standards. Along with Australia, Canada, and Germany, the United States is different from most other countries in having little national or federal control of education. Countries such as France and Japan that have strong education ministries can set forth curriculum content and standards for schools. If Japanese students move from Sendai to Kyoto or Tokyo, their new teachers will know what they studied in previous grades. The United States is only now fitfully and variously enacting state standards. Many teachers do not know what their students previously learned even if they remain in the same school, district, or state. For this reason, American teachers spend much of the first part of each academic year in review of prerequisite knowledge and skills, which bores some children and excessively challenges others.

Even fully enacted state standards might not solve the problem. About one-fifth of U.S. families move each year, some from state to state. Sharply defined and different standards from state to state could make school transitions even harder for such children. One solution is to test them and possibly hold them back a semester or a grade. Efforts by subject matter experts, educators, and members of the public to specify grade-level content standards in mathematics, history, and English are hardly encouraging; they have been unable to reach a stable national consensus on what should be taught much less seeing that it is widely and uniformly enacted in schools.

National for-profit firms and not-for-profit groups such as Edison Schools, Core Knowledge, and Sabis provide some hope, since they have developed curricula that are uniformly employed in their respective schools. In more than a merely futuristic sense, the Internet and other forms of distance education provide a promising means of delivering "anytime, anyplace" uniform content that is well articulated from grade to grade or from learning experience to learning experience.

Related to grade articulation is "aligned time on task," which means that teaching and study time should reflect curricular goals. Students who are actively engaged in activities focused on specific instructional goals make more progress toward these goals. Alignment of assessment with curricular goals can also provide time efficiency. "Systemic reform" means that three components of the curriculum—goals; textbooks, other teaching materials, and learning activities; and tests and other outcome assessments—are well matched in content and emphasis. Consequently, students at a given grade level should have greater degrees of shared knowledge and skills as prerequisites for further learning; teachers can avoid excessive review; and progress can be better assessed.

PEDAGOGICAL METHODS

Evidence from many studies of 275 pedagogical methods and educational conditions are summarized elsewhere.[3] This section concerns several that are relatively simple to employ and that have excellent records of promoting learning. The research on these methods and conditions has accumulated over half a century. Most of the studies employed control-groups and contrasted the amount learned, or gains, from pretests to posttests given before and after the intervention. Other studies analyzed national and international achievement surveys of as many as several hundred thousand students.

Parent Involvement

Learning is enhanced when schools encourage parents to stimulate their children's intellectual development. Dozens of studies in the United States, Australia, Canada, England, and elsewhere show that the home environment powerfully

---

[3]Ibid.

influences what children and youth learn within and outside school. This environment is considerably more powerful than the parents' income and education in influencing what children learn in the first six years of life and during the twelve years of primary and secondary education.

As previously mentioned, one major reason that parental influence is potentially so strong is that from birth through age eighteen children spend approximately 87 percent of their waking hours outside school under the nominal or real influence of their parents. Cooperative efforts by parents and educators to modify alterable conditions in the home have strong, beneficial effects on learning. In twenty-nine controlled studies, 91 percent of the comparisons favored children in such programs over nonparticipant control groups.

Sometimes called "the curriculum of the home," the home environment refers to informed parent-child conversations about school and everyday events; encouragement and discussion of leisure reading; monitoring and critical review of television viewing and peer activities; deferral of immediate gratification to accomplish long-term goals; expressions of affection and interest in the child's academic and other progress as a person; and perhaps, among such unremitting efforts, laughter and caprice. Reading to children and discussing everyday events prepare them for academic activities before attending school.

Cooperation between educators and parents can support these approaches. Educators can suggest specific activities likely to stimulate children's learning at home and in school. They can also develop and organize large-scale teacher-parent programs to systematically promote academically stimulating conditions and activities outside school.

Graded Homework

Students learn more when they complete homework that is graded, commented on, and discussed by their teachers. A synthesis of more than a dozen studies of the effects of homework in various subjects showed that the assignment and completion of homework yields positive effects on academic achievement. The effects are almost tripled when teachers take time to grade the work, make corrections and specific comments on improvements that can be made, and discuss problems and solutions with individual students or the whole class. Homework also seems particularly effective in high school.

Like a three-legged stool, homework requires a teacher to assign it and provide feedback, a parent to monitor it, and a student to do it. If one leg is weak, the stool may fall down. The role of the teacher in providing feedback—in reinforcing what has been done correctly and in reteaching what has not—is key to maximizing the positive impact of homework.

Districts and schools that have well-known homework policies for daily minutes of required work are likely to reap benefits. Homework "hotlines" in which students may call in for help have proven useful. To relieve some of the workload of grading, teachers can employ procedures in which students grade their own and other students' work. In this way, they can learn cooperative social skills and how to evaluate their own and others' efforts.

The quality of homework is as important as the amount. Effective homework is relevant to the lessons to be learned and in keeping with students' abilities.

Direct Teaching

Many studies show that direct teaching can be effective in promoting student learning. It emphasizes systematic sequencing of lessons, a presentation of new content and skills, guided student practice, feedback, and independent practice by students. The traits of teachers employing effective direct instruction include clarity, task orientation, enthusiasm, and flexibility. Effective direct teachers also clearly organize their presentations and occasionally use student ideas.

The use of direct teaching can be traced to the turn of the century; it is what many citizens and parents expect to see in classrooms. Done well, it can yield consistent and substantial results. The usual aspects of direct teaching are as follows:

- Daily review, homework check, and, if necessary, reteaching
- Presentation of new content and skills in small steps
- Guided student practice with close teacher monitoring
- Corrective feedback and instructional reinforcement
- Independent practice in seatwork and homework with a high (more than 90 percent) success rate
- Weekly and monthly reviews

Organized Lessons

Showing students the relationships between past learning and present learning increases its depth and breadth. More than a dozen studies show that when teachers explain how new ideas in the current lesson relate to ideas in previous lessons and other prior learning, students can connect the old with the new, which helps them better remember and understand. Similarly, alerting them learn key points allows them to concentrate on the most crucial parts of the lessons.

Well-organized lessons enable students to focus on key ideas and concentrate on the relations among them. Moreover, understanding the sequential or logical continuity of subject matter can be motivating. If students simply learn one isolated idea after another, the subject matter may appear arbitrary. But having a "mental road map" of what they have accomplished, where they are presently, and where they are going can help them avoid unpleasant surprises and set realistic goals. Similar effects can be accomplished by goal setting, overviewing, and pretesting that sensitizes students to important points and questions in textbooks and by teachers.

It may also be useful to show students that what they are learning solves problems that exist in the world outside school, problems they are likely to encounter in life. For example, human biology that features nutrition and exercise applications is likely to be more interesting than molecular biology, at least for beginning students. Teachers and textbooks can sometimes make effective use of graphic organizers. Maps, timetables, flow charts depicting the sequence of activities, and other such devices may be worth hundreds of words. They may also be easier to remember.

Learning Strategies

Giving students some choice in their learning goals and teaching them to be attentive to their progress can yield learning gains. In the 1980s, reformers sought ways to encourage self-monitoring, self-teaching, or "meta-cognition" to foster both achievement and independence. They viewed skills as important, but the learner's monitoring and management of his or her own learning had primacy, since citizens in democratic societies are expected to learn and think for themselves. This approach transfers to learners part of the direct teaching functions of planning, allocating time, and review. Being aware of what goes on in one's mind during learning is a critical first step to effective independent learning.

Some students lack this self-awareness and must be taught the skills necessary to monitor and regulate their own learning. Many studies have demonstrated that positive effects can accrue from developed skills. Such effort can be premature and overdone, however, since it would be wasteful to expect students to rediscover large parts of knowledge on their own.

Students with a repertoire of learning strategies can measure their own progress toward explicit goals. When students use these strategies to strengthen their opportunities for learning, they increase their knowledge as well as their sense of self-control and positive self-evaluation.

Three possible phases of teaching about learning strategies are as follows:

- Modeling, in which the teacher exhibits the desired behavior
- Guided practice, in which students perform with help from the teacher
- Application, in which students act independently of the teacher

As an example, a successful program of "reciprocal teaching" fosters reading comprehension by having students take turns in leading dialogues on pertinent features of texts. By assuming the roles of planning, preparation, and monitoring ordinarily exercised by teachers, students can learn self-management and how to collaborate as well as gain knowledge and skills. Perhaps that is why tutors learn from tutoring and why it is said, "To learn something well, teach it."

Tutoring and Computer-Assisted Instruction

Teaching a single student or a small number with the same abilities and instructional needs can be remarkably effective because such tutoring suits learning to student needs. It has yielded large learning effects in several dozen studies. It yields particularly large effects in mathematics—perhaps because of the subject's well-defined sequence and organization. If students fall behind in a fast-paced mathematics class, they may never catch up unless their particular problems are identified and remedied.

The process of individualized assessment and remediation is a virtue of tutoring and other means of adapting instruction to an individual learner's needs. Computer-assisted instruction, for example, has a long history of success for the same reason.

Tutoring of slower or younger students by more advanced students appears to work nearly as well as teacher tutoring; with sustained student practice, it might be equal to teacher tutoring in some cases. Still, it is possible to abuse this technique, and advanced students need the significant challenge of their own peers.

Peer tutoring among equals also can promote effective learning, in tutors as well as tutees. Organizing one's thoughts to impart them intelligibly to others, becoming conscious of the value of time, and learning managerial and social skills are some of the side benefits for tutors.

Even slower-learning students and those with disabilities can teach others if they are given the extra time and practice that may be required to master specialized knowledge or skills. This can give them a positive experience and increase their feelings of self-esteem. Again, moderation may be crucial.

CONDITIONS FOR EFFECTIVE TEACHING

The methods described in the last section are hardly astonishing. They reflect not only research findings but also common sense and personal experiences we may have had with our better teachers. What is astonishing is that they are so seldom practiced or well practiced. Because policy makers, citizens, and parents now more fully realize both the need and the potential to raise achievement substantially, they need to know about what promotes good teaching methods. Unfortunately, the research on this important matter is neither voluminous nor as rigorous as the control-group studies on teaching methods. Some expert syntheses, large-scale surveys, and case studies of outstanding schools that attain exceptional achievement do provide useful and promising insights.

Indicators of School Quality

The National Society of School Evaluation (NSSE) is the research arm of regional-school accrediting groups such as the New England Association. A few years ago, the NSSE sought from leading authorities the school features and activities associated with high levels of achievement. Translated into observable indicators, these are shown in Table 2.

TABLE 2   Indicators of School Quality Associated with Achievement

A. Curriculum
   1. Develops quality curriculum
   2. Ensures effective implementation and articulation of curriculum
   3. Evaluates and renews the curriculum
B. Instructional design
   1. Aligns instruction with goals
   2. Employs data-driven instructional decision making
   3. Actively engages students in their learning
   4. Expands instructional support for student learning
C. Assessment
   1. Clearly defines the expectations for student learning
   2. Establishes the purpose of assessment
   3. Selects the appropriate method of assessment
   4. Collects a comprehensive and representative sample of student achievement
   5. Develops fair assessments and avoids bias and distortion
D. Educational agenda
   1. Facilitates a collaborative process in developing a shared vision
   2. Develops a shared vision, beliefs, and mission
   3. Defines measurable goals focused on students' learning
E. Leadership for school improvement
   1. Promotes quality instruction by fostering an academic learning climate
   2. Develops schoolwide plans for improvement
   3. Employs effective decision making
   4. Monitors progress in improving student achievement and instructional effectiveness
   5. Provides skillful stewardship
F. Community building
   1. Fosters community-building conditions within the school
   2. Extends the school community through collaborative networks and improvement
G. Continuous improvement and learning
   1. Builds skills and capacity for improvement through comprehensive and ongoing professional development
   2. Creates the conditions that support productive change

These indicators can serve educators and school boards that want to assess their programs. The NSSE provides the more detailed indicators, forms, and procedures for self-assessment.

Successful Schools for Students in Poverty

Students in poverty are often low academic achievers. These students are more often subject to premature birth, low birth weight, and early stress and disease. Their mothers are more often teens, single, or divorced; they move more frequently. They may be less able to provide the experiences and child-rearing practices associated with academic achievement, such as leisure reading and vocabulary building. For this reason, Gordon Cawelti[4] studied six high-performing schools around the country that seemed to overcome such risks of achievement failure. The schools shared the following features:

- There is a focus on clear standards and on improving results.
- Teamwork helps ensure accountability.
- The principal is a strong leader.
- Teachers are deeply committed to helping all students achieve.
- Multiple changes are made to improve the instructional life of students, and these efforts are sustained in concert.

Competitive and Cost-Effective Private Schools

Although U.S. schools make the least progress in reading, mathematics, and science during the school years, the per-student costs of their schools are third-highest among two dozen economically advanced countries. Market theorists

---

[4]Gordon Cawelti, *Portraits of Six Benchmark Schools: Diverse Approaches to Improving Student Achievement* (Alexandria, Va.: Educational Research Service, 1999).

believe that the lack of competition among public schools is their downfall. In this view, private schools that must charge tuition and compete in the marketplace for students should not only be more effective but also more cost-efficient.

Although this hypothesis is not restricted to Catholic schools, most of the research has focused on them. There are more of them, and they often have cost data and uniform standardized testing. This allows comparison with public schools in their neighborhoods that serve students from the same socioeconomic and ethnic backgrounds. Sociologists and economists who study this question also try to control for such things as parent motivation, education, and other factors.

In my view, the clear weight of the evidence suggests that, other things being equal, students in Catholic schools, many of whom are minorities and not Catholic, do better and that the costs are less than half those of public schools even when special education students and their costs are omitted from the analysis. Valerie Lee[5] identified the distinctive features of Catholic schools that yield such efficiency:

A. A delimited core curriculum followed by all students, regardless of their family background, academic preparation, or future educational plans
B. Caring organization
   1. Frequent opportunities for face-to-face interactions and shared experiences among adults and students
   2. Common curriculum and school events—athletics, drama, music
   3. Teachers see responsibilities beyond classroom subject matter—extending into hallways, school grounds, neighborhood, and homes
   4. Shared beliefs about what students should learn

---

[5]Valerie Lee, "Catholic Lessons for Public Schools," in Diane Ravitch, ed., *New Schools for a New Century* (New Haven, Conn.: Yale University Press): 147–163.

C. Decentralized governance
 1. Small central office for the system
 2. Principal has considerable control over daily operations
 3. Principal selected from faculty
 4. Important decisions made at the school site

We might also expect efficiency from ordinary Jewish, Lutheran, and other parochial and independent schools that must compete for urban students in the marketplace.

Turning Around the Chicago System

When U.S. Secretary of Education Bill Bennett declared the Chicago public schools the worst in the nation, the district had a miserable track record. Eighty-four percent of the district's children were in poverty, and the district contained 80 percent of the state's bilingual children. Chicago had suffered eight teacher strikes in fifteen years, had a continuing financial crisis, and saw an enrollment decline of 29 percent, to 433,000 students—all of which united parents, citizens, and business leaders.

In response, the Illinois legislature forbade a teacher strike for five years and allowed Mayor Richard Daley to appoint his own board and top staff, including Chief Executive Officer Paul Vallas and Chief Education Officer Cozette Buckney. Under board direction, they simultaneously made achievement the clear priority; imposed rigorous accountability on principals, teachers, and students; vastly enlarged private competitive contracting; and granted charters to publicly funded, privately governed schools.[6]

The mayoral team members terminated 2,000 nonteaching positions and transferred the savings to schools for direct student services. They soon terminated 36 principals for failure to progress. Teachers from "reconstituted" failing

---

[6]Richard P. Niemiec and Herbert J. Walberg, eds., *Evaluating Chicago School Reform: New Directions in Program Evaluation, a Publication of the American Evaluation Association* (San Francisco: Jossey-Bass, 1993).

schools were replaced by a new staff and had ten months to find another job in the system or face unemployment. For Chicago's many poorly prepared teachers, the team provided lesson plans developed by skilled teachers.

The team transferred to alternative schools students who had twenty unexcused absences, records of assaults, or records of carrying weapons. As mentioned earlier, students falling sufficiently behind their grade levels were given the choice of grade retention or trying to make up for poor achievement in intensive summer schools. The results were as follows:

- Three years of rising test scores in all subjects
- Attendance at 90 percent for the first time in fifteen years
- Truancy cut in half
- Enrollment up by about 30,000 students

This results-oriented, businesslike, "tough love" approach has become a model for other city systems. The Chicago leadership recently announced that it would begin grading parents for their efforts, and the school board has allowed charter schools to flourish. If they can provide models and competition for other conventionally governed schools, so much the better.

Successful State Initiatives

Finally, states can create the conditions for improved teaching and learning. For the National Education Goals Panel, David Grissmer and Ann Flanagan carried out case studies of Texas and North Carolina, states that stood out in making gains on the National Assessment of Educational Progress examinations, in reducing the achievement gap between disadvantaged and other students, and in spending less per pupil than did other states. How did they do it?

The states were similar to one another, and their experiences parallel some of the findings already described. They created statewide-aligned systems of standards, curriculum, and assessments. They held schools accountable for improvement by all students. They achieved critical support from business in developing and sustaining changes over time. They provided financial rewards for schools based on performance and could disenfranchise school districts and remove principals because of poor performance.

The researchers speculated that such conditions caused more specific teaching objectives and that teachers increased the time and attention devoted to achieving the learning standards. They concluded that several reforms implemented by other states make for no difference in better achievement, namely, per-pupil spending, teacher/pupil ratios, teachers with advanced degrees, and experience levels of teachers.

CONCLUSION

Effective teaching methods hardly seem a mystery. Much research bears out the commonsense principles many of us saw our better teachers practice. To solve the American achievement problem, we need to take these principles seriously. We need to put them into practice with respect to the amount of time students study within and outside their classes. We need to organize the subject matter so that it's conveyed clearly and efficiently. And we need good pedagogy.

The mystery seems to be why such principles are not already in place. But it is becoming clear that school, district, and state policies can encourage the implementation of effective principles. These policies include setting achievement priorities; establishing and aligning goals, content, and tests; measuring results; and holding the chief players accountable. In turn, these policies may require (1) carrots and sticks or (2) parent choice of schools, including public, parochial, and independent for-profit and not-for-profit all competing for customers or (3) both.

Appendix: Conference Agenda

Hoover Institution—Pacific Research Institute

Teacher Quality Conference
Stauffer Auditorium, Hoover Institution, Stanford, May 12, 2000

8:00 AM	**Continental Breakfast and Registration**
8:30 AM	**Introductory Remarks** John Raisian, Director, Hoover Institution, and Sally Pipes, Pacific Research Institute
8:45 AM	**The Academic Literature and Teacher Quality** Professor Eric Hanushek, University of Rochester
9:30 AM	**Value-Added Research** June Rivers, coauthor with Professor William Sanders of University of Tennessee, Knoxville
10:15 AM	**Coffee Break**
10:30 AM	**Teacher Quality Accountability Systems** Dr. Eugene Hickok, Secretary of Education, Commonwealth of Pennsylvania
11:15 AM	**Teacher Training and Pedagogical Methods** Professor J. E. Stone, East Tennessee State University
12:00 PM	**Lunch**
1:00 PM	**Teaching Methodologies** Professor Herbert Walberg, University of Illinois, Chicago
1:45 PM	**Concluding Remarks** Hoover/Pacific Research Institute
Respondent:	Tom Loveless, Brookings Institution

Editors and Contributors

WILLIAM J. BENNETT was U.S. Secretary of Education and Chairman of the National Endowment for the Humanities under President Reagan and Director of the Office of National Drug Control Policy under President George H. W. Bush. The author of *The Book of Virtues* and several other bestsellers, he is a fellow at the Heritage Foundation and codirector of Empower America. He is founder and Chairman of K–12, an Internet-based school for kindergarten through twelfth grade.

WILLIAMSON M. EVERS is a research fellow at Stanford University's Hoover Institution and a member of the Institution's Koret Task Force on K–12 Education. Dr. Evers is a member of the National Educational Research Policy and Priorities Board and the White House Commission on Presidential Scholars. He currently serves on the California state testing system's question-writing panels for history and mathematics and served on the California State Academic Standards Commission. He is a member of the board of directors of the East Palo Alto Charter School and a member of the policy board of the California History–Social Science Project, which provides subject-matter training to teachers.

ERIC A. HANUSHEK is the Paul and Jean Hanna Senior Fellow on Education Policy at the Hoover Institution. His research concentrates on applied public finance and public policy analysis with special emphasis on education issues. From 1983 through 1985, Dr. Hanushek was deputy director of the Congressional Budget Office. He was president of the Association for Public Policy Analysis and Management in 1988–89. In 1997, he was selected to be a member of the International Academy of Education.

EUGENE W. HICKOK is U.S. Undersecretary of Education. From 1995 to 2001, he served as Pennsylvania Secretary of Education. Before that, he served as associate professor of political science at Dickinson College in Pennsylvania.

LANCE T. IZUMI is senior fellow in California studies and director of the Center for School Reform at the Pacific Research Institute for Public Policy. He is the author of several major studies, including the California Index of Leading Education Indicators (1997 and 2000 editions). He serves as a commissioner on the California Postsecondary Education Commission and is a member of the Professional Development Working Group of the California Legislature's Joint Committee to Develop a Master Plan for Education.

JUNE C. RIVERS is the assistant manager of value-added assessment and research for SAS inSchool. Dr. Rivers has collaborated with Dr. William Sanders on research on the influence of school systems, schools, and teachers on student performance. Dr. Rivers has also served as a K–12 teacher and administrator, a member of the Tennessee education commissioner's staff, and a staff member of the University of Tennessee State Testing and Evaluation Center.

WILLIAM L. SANDERS is the manager of value-added assessment and research for SAS inSchool. Previously, he served as professor and director of the University of Tennessee Value-Added Research and Assessment Center. Research conducted by Dr. Sanders and his colleagues demonstrated that value-added education outcome assessment can be measured from student achievement data.

J. E. STONE is a professor of education psychology at East Tennessee State University. He is the author of numerous scholarly and popular articles on teaching methodology, and he edits and operates the Education Consumers Clearinghouse Web site (www.education-consumers.com).

HERBERT J. WALBERG is a research professor of education and psychology at the University of Illinois at Chicago. His research focuses on the effects of various education conditions and methods on learning and other outcomes. He has prepared comparative education studies for the U.S. Department of Education, the Department of State, and the White House. Dr. Walberg served on the National Assessment Governing Board and is a fellow of four academic organizations, including the American Association for the Advancement of Science, the American Psychological Association, and the Royal Statistical Society. Walberg is founding member and vice president of the International Academy of Education, headquartered in Brussels. He chaired the scientific advisory group for the Paris-based Organization for Economic Cooperation and Development, a project on international educational indicators. He currently chairs the board of Chicago's Heartland Institute.

Index

Academic Development Institute, 58

Academic growth rate: Tennessee value-added assessment system, 14–18

Accountability, 8–9, 19, 72; in Pennsylvania, 27

American Council on Education, 51

American Federation of Teachers, 51

Attribute-treatment interaction studies, 43

Bennett, William J., ix, 70, 73

Best practice teaching. *See* Learner-centered instruction

Book of Virtues, The, 73

Buckney, Cozette, 70

Burroughs, R., 51

Bush, George H. W., 73, 74

California class-size reduction policy of 1997, 7, 10

Carnine, D., 44

Carter, Samuel Casey, 34

Catholic schools: expenditures, 69; features of, 69–70; students in, 69

Cawelti, Gordon, 56, 68

Charter schools, 31

Chicago public schools: problems with, 70; successful reforms in, 70–71

Cizek, Gregory J., 56

Class-size reduction, 25, 43; effectiveness of, 44; implications of, 7; as input policy, 5; and Project STAR, 6; resources devoted to, 5–6; results of, 6

Coleman Report, 2

Collins, C., 38

Committee on Assessment and Teacher Quality, 50

Constructivism, 40

Consumers: beliefs held by, 40; vs. educators, 36–41; relation to schools, 36; and teacher assessment, 50–51

Core Knowledge, 59

Curriculum: uniform standards, 59–60

Daley, Richard, 70

Daniels, H., 38, 39

Darling-Hammond, L., 42

Dawson, Thomas, III, xvi

Diagnosis, 19
Direct Instruction (DI), 48; de-
    scription, 45; results, 45
Direct teaching: aspects of, 63;
    effectiveness, 62
Duffett, A., 39

Edison Schools, 59
Education: conceptual differences
    between educators and con-
    sumers on, 37–41; con-
    sumers (see Consumers);
    Direct Instruction (DI), 45;
    divide in, 29; equity in, 14;
    and learner-centered instruc-
    tion, 44–45; productivity
    factors, 57; specialists in, 44
Educational Empowerment Act,
    26–27; supporters of, 27
Educational process: and legis-
    lation, 7
Education Consumers Clearing-
    House, 35, 36
Education Consumers Consul-
    tants Network, 36
Edutainment, 45
Ethnicity: and the TVAAS find-
    ings, 17
Evers, Williamson M., xiii, 73
Expenditures, 71, 72; in Catholic
    schools, 69; per student,
    68. See also Resources

Family background: and
    teacher quality, 3
Farkas, G., 39
Federal government: and per-
    formance incentive systems,
    9; and policy making, 7
Finn, C., 48, 54
Flanagan, Ann, 71
Follow Through Project, 47
Frantz, D., 38

Griffin, G., 42
Grissmer, David, 71

Haertel, Geneva D., 56
Hanushek, Eric A., ix, x, xiv, 1,
    25, 44, 73–74, 77
Harville, D. A., 16
Hendricks-Lee, M., 51
Heritage Foundation, 34
Hickock, Eugene W., xv, 25,
    74, 77
Hill, D., 53, 54
Hirsch, E. D., 42
Holmes, Oliver Wendell, x
Home environment, 61
Homework, 61–62; effects of, 62;
    participants, 62; tools, 62
Hoover Institution, vii, viii, ix,
    xi, xiii, xiv, xvi
Horn, S.P., 15, 16, 17, 19
Hyde, A., 38, 39

Immerwahr, J., 37
Incentives: approaches to, 8;
    and criteria for rewards,
    9; experimenting with,
    10–11; and local school
    districts, 9–10; in Pennsyl-
    vania, 30; role of, in pol-
    icy making, 30
Inner-city schools. See Urban
    education
Input policies: evidence on, 5–6;
    implications of, 6–7; and
    smaller class size, 5
INTASC. See Interstate New
    Teacher Assessment and
    Support Consortium
Internet, 59–60
Interstate New Teacher Assess-
    ment and Support Consor-
    tium, 48, 50
Izumi, Lance T., xiii, 74

Jennings, T., 39
Johnson, J., 37, 39
Johnson, J. E., 45
Johnson, K. M., 45
Jordan, H. R., 16

Kanstoroom, M., 48, 54

Lai, Jin-Shei, 56
Learner-centered instruction,
    44–45; and constructivism,
    40; description of, 39–40;
    emphasis of, 40; purpose
    of, 40; reason for failures
    of, 41; and student diversity
    awareness, 42–43; and
    teacher examinations,
    50–51
Learning: causes of, 56–57; and
    direct teaching, 62–63;
    and home environment,
    61; and organized lessons,
    63–64; strategies, 64–65;
    and uniform content, 60
Lee, Valerie, 69
Local school districts: measur-
    ing effectiveness of, 20–21;
    obtaining data for, 19
Loveless, Tom, 77

McClure, R., 42
Measurement: and decreasing
    variability of teacher effec-
    tiveness, 21–22; purpose
    of, 19, 22–23
Mendro, R. L., 16
Merit pay: in England, 10
Meta-cognition, 64
Millman, J., 15

NAEYC. *See* National Associa-
    tion for the Education of
    Young Children

National Assessment of Educa-
    tional Progress, 71
National Association for the
    Education of Young Chil-
    dren (NAEYC), 46
National Board of Professional
    Teaching Standards
    (NBPTS), 48, 50, 51
National Center for Education
    Statistics, 51
National Commission on
    Teaching and America's
    Future (NCTAF), 42, 48;
    strategy of, 49–50
National Council for the Accredi-
    tation of Teacher Education
    (NCATE), 42, 48, 49, 50
National Education Goals
    Panel, 71
National Society of School
    Evaluation (NSSE), 66
National Teachers Examina-
    tion, 50
NBPTS. *See* National Board of
    Professional Teaching
    Standards
NCATE. *See* National Council
    for the Accreditation of
    Teacher Education
NCTAF. *See* National Commis-
    sion on Teaching and
    America's Future
NCTAF initiative, 48
Niemiec, Richard P., 70
"No Excuses" schools, 34
NSSE. *See* National Society of
    School Evaluation

Open Education model, 47

Pacific Research Institute for
    Public Policy (PRI), vii,
    viii, ix, xi, xiii, xvi

Parental influence, 61
Pedagogical effectiveness: evidence regarding, 45–46
Pedagogical methods: and computer-assisted instruction, 65; and direct teaching, 62–63; and graded homework, 61–62; and learning strategies, 64–65; and organized lessons, 63–64; and parent involvement, 60–61; and tutoring, 65
Pedagogy: background of mainstream, 42; core curriculum in, 51; methods of (*see* Pedagogical methods); and NCTAF-inspired reforms, 49
Pennsylvania: alternative certification programs in, 28; educational system in, 26; and incentive programs, 30; and low-performing districts, 27; new teacher-preparation standards in, 28–29; professional development in, 30–31; tenure in, 28
Performance: measurement, 9
Pipes, Sally, vii, xvi, 77
Policy making: and equity in education, 18; role of incentives in, 30; and teacher requirements, 4; and value-added assessment, 52
Poverty, 34
Praxis, 50
Professional development: in Pennsylvania, 30–31
Project Follow Through, 45
Project STAR, 6
Public Agenda, 29

Raisian, John, vii, xvi, 77
Ravitch, Diane, 56, 69
Reagan, Ronald, 73
Reforms: and Pennsylvania teacher-preparation standards, 28–29; systemic, 60
Resources: and performance, 6; for U.S. education since 1960, 5–6; use of, 8
Result-oriented methods, 44
Reynolds, Arthur J., 56
Ridge, Tom, xv, 25, 26, 27
Rivers, June C. *See* Rivers-Sanders, June C.
Rivers-Sanders, June C., ix, xiv, xv, 13, 16, 17, 33, 74, 77
Roe, T., 51

Sabis, 59
Sanders, William L., ix, xiv, xv, 13, 15, 16, 17, 19, 53, 74, 77
Saxton, A. M., 15, 16
Schools: and consumers, 35–36; cost of, 68; indicators of quality, 67; "No Excuses," 34; poverty and success in, 68; private (Catholic), 69
Self-esteem: Open Education model, 47; and student performance, 47
Snow, R., 43
Standard and Poors, 31
Stone, J. E., xv, 33, 37, 52, 54, 75, 77; background, 35–36
Student performance, 8, 35
Students: in Asia, 58; in Catholic schools, 69; differences in, 43; and learning, 56; learning awareness of, 64–65; and organized lessons, 63–64; poor study habits of, 58; in poverty, 68; and

results of ineffective teaching, 21, 22; self-esteem of, 47; and tutoring, 65–66
Study time: in Asia, 58; in the United States, 58
Swanson, J., 43
Systemic reform, 60

Taube, Tad, viii, xvi
Teacher certification requirements, 4–5; increasing, 6–7
Teacher certification standards: in Pennsylvania, 28
Teacher quality, 2, 25; assessing, 51–52; definition of, 3; family background and, 3; and findings from the TVAAS on, 16–18; and increasing requirements, 6–7; measuring, 3, 9; problems with, 48–49; and progress in Pennsylvania, 29
Teachers: assessing, 50–51; in Chicago's public schools, 70–71; conflicting demands imposed on, 29–30; vs. consumers, 36–41; and Direct Instruction, 45; and diversity among students, 43; effectiveness, 18, 19; inexperienced, 22; job security, 27; objective assessment of, 53; performance data on, 54; performance incentives for, 8 (*see also* Incentives); quality (*see* Teacher quality); role of, 32; shrinking effectiveness variability of, 21; specialized, 43–44; training and effectiveness, 34; and uniform standards, 59–60

Teacher training, 33–34, 51; and the Education Consumers Consultants Network, 36; programs, 49; reforms, 46–47, 48; respecting consumers, 52; and teacher effectiveness, 34
Teaching: amount of, 57–58; computer-assisted, 65; conditions for effective, 66–72; direct, 62–63; and the Internet, 59–60; reciprocal, 65; tutoring, 65
Teaching methods: choosing, 56; and nine educational productivity factors, 57
Tennessee value-added assessment system (TVAAS), 34, 53, 54; and accountability, 19–20; advantages of, 15; description of, 14–15; pertinent findings of, 16–18
Tenure: in Pennsylvania, 28
Testing instruments, 19
Title I funds, 12
Title II of the 1998 Higher Education Act, 54
Tutoring: effectiveness, 65; peer, 65–66
TVAAS. *See* Tennessee value-added assessment system

Urban education, 22, 27; and Chicago public schools, 58, 70–71
U.S. Department of Education, 51

Vallas, Paul, 70
Value-added assessment, 8–9, 34; of a novice teacher, 52; objectivity of, 53; and policy makers, 52–53; Tennessee system of, 14–18

Walberg, Herbert J., x, xiv,
   55, 56, 57, 70, 74,
   77
Walt Disney World, 38
Watkins, C. L., 45
Waxman, Hersholt C., 56

Weerasinghe, D., 16
Whole child, 44
Wise, A., 42
Wright, S. P., 17

Zemelman, S., 38, 39